Christmas

IN THE COUNTRY

Edited by Laura Scott

HOUSE of
WHITE
BIRCHES

PUBLISHERS
SINCE 1947

Editor: Laura Scott
Associate Editor: June Sprunger
Copy Editor: Cathy Reef
Photography: Nora Elsesser, Tammy Christian, Arlou Wittwer
Photography Assistant: Linda Quinlan

Production Manager: Vicki Macy
Creative Coordinator: Shaun Venish
Book Design/Production: Becky Sarasin
Traffic Coordinator: Sandra Beres
Production Assistants: Dana Brotherton, Cheryl Lynch,
Darren Powell, Jessica Rothe, Miriam Zacharias
Watercolor Illustrations: Vicki Macy

Publishers: Carl H. Muselman, Arthur K. Muselman
Chief Executive Officer: John Robinson
Marketing Director: Scott Moss
Editorial Director: Vivian Rothe
Production Director: Scott Smith

Printed in the United States of America
First Printing: 1997
Library of Congress Number: 97-71138
ISBN: 1-882138-26-0

Every effort has been made to ensure the accuracy and completeness of the instructions in this book. However, we cannot be responsible for human error or for the results when using materials other than those specified in the instructions, or for variations in individual work.

Cover project: *Christmas Goose Centerpiece,* page 112

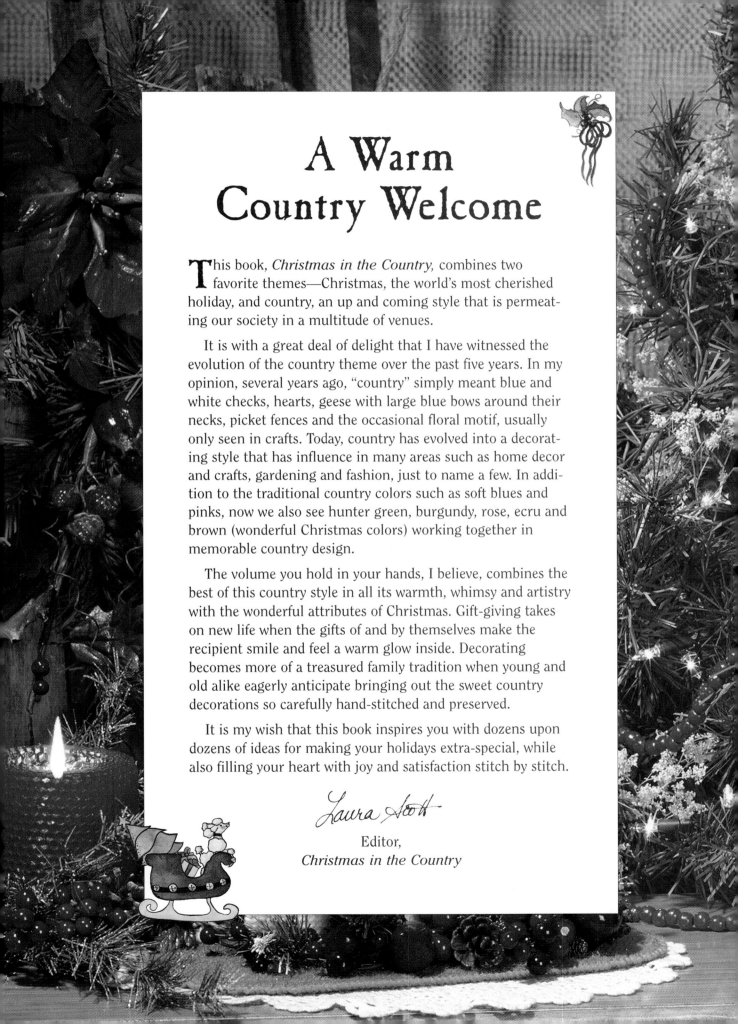

A Warm Country Welcome

This book, *Christmas in the Country*, combines two favorite themes—Christmas, the world's most cherished holiday, and country, an up and coming style that is permeating our society in a multitude of venues.

It is with a great deal of delight that I have witnessed the evolution of the country theme over the past five years. In my opinion, several years ago, "country" simply meant blue and white checks, hearts, geese with large blue bows around their necks, picket fences and the occasional floral motif, usually only seen in crafts. Today, country has evolved into a decorating style that has influence in many areas such as home decor and crafts, gardening and fashion, just to name a few. In addition to the traditional country colors such as soft blues and pinks, now we also see hunter green, burgundy, rose, ecru and brown (wonderful Christmas colors) working together in memorable country design.

The volume you hold in your hands, I believe, combines the best of this country style in all its warmth, whimsy and artistry with the wonderful attributes of Christmas. Gift-giving takes on new life when the gifts of and by themselves make the recipient smile and feel a warm glow inside. Decorating becomes more of a treasured family tradition when young and old alike eagerly anticipate bringing out the sweet country decorations so carefully hand-stitched and preserved.

It is my wish that this book inspires you with dozens upon dozens of ideas for making your holidays extra-special, while also filling your heart with joy and satisfaction stitch by stitch.

Laura Scott

Editor,
Christmas in the Country

Contents

Treasures for the Tree

Gifts for All

Holiday Entertaining

Dressing Up the Mantel

Festive Decor

Let It Snow!

Treasures For the Tree

Mini Mittens
Instructions begin on page 8

Mini Mittens

A cuddly bear, cheery snowman and sweet doll pop out of the cuffs of three delightful mitten ornaments, while colorful plaid ribbon, gold jingle bells and soft pompons adorn a coordinating ornament-and-pin pair. See photo on page 6.

Skill Level
Beginner

Materials
- Small amount 7-count plastic canvas
- Small amount 10-count plastic canvas
- Coats & Clark Red Heart Super Saver Art. E301 worsted weight yarn as listed in color key
- DMC #3 pearl cotton as listed in color key
- ½" white pompon
- ¾" white pompon
- 1½" gold pin back
- 6mm gold jingle bell
- 9mm gold jingle bell
- Scrap ⅛"-wide red satin ribbon
- 6" ⅜"-wide red-and-green plaid ribbon
- Low-temperature glue gun

Snowball Mittens

Instructions

1. Cut one mitten and one cuff from 7-count plastic canvas and one mitten and one cuff from 10-count plastic canvas according to graphs.

2. Stitch 7-count plastic canvas with worsted weight yarn and 10-count plastic canvas with #3 pearl cotton following graphs. Overcast 7-count pieces with paddy green and 10-count pieces with medium emerald green.

3. Cut one 3" length and one 1½" length from medium emerald green pearl cotton. Glue the ends of 3" length to the upper right-hand corner of the 7-count mitten front, forming a loop. Repeat with 1½" length on 10-count mitten.

4. Glue corresponding cuffs to mitten tops over ends of loops. Using photo as a guide through step 6, glue large pompon to large mitten and small pompon to small mitten.

Continue pattern

Snowball Mitten
17 holes x 19 holes
Cut 1 from 7-count
Stitch with yarn
Cut 1 from 10-count
Stitch with pearl cotton

COLOR KEY	
SNOWBALL MITTENS	
Worsted Weight Yarn	**Yards**
☐ Spring green #367	2
■ Paddy green #368	4
#3 Pearl Cotton	
☐ Nile #913	2
■ Medium emerald green #911	4
Color numbers given are for Coats & Clark Red Heart Super Saver worsted weight yarn Art. E301 and DMC #3 pearl cotton.	

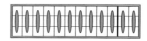

Snowball Mitten Cuff
12 holes x 3 holes
Cut 1 from 7-count
Stitch with yarn
Cut 1 from 10-count
Stitch with pearl cotton

5. For small mitten, make a small bow with red ribbon and glue to right side of mitten under cuff. Glue 6mm bell just under center bottom of bow. Glue pin back to center back of mitten.

6. For large mitten, make a two- or four-loop bow from plaid ribbon. Thread matching color of pearl cotton through jingle bell; wrap pearl cotton around center of bow. Glue bow to right side of mitten under cuff.

Doll, Snowman & Teddy Bear Mittens

Skill Level
Beginner

Materials
- ½ sheet 10-count plastic canvas
- DMC #3 pearl cotton as listed in color key
- DMC 6-strand embroidery floss as listed in color key

- Small amount ⅛"-wide satin ribbon: green and burgundy
- 6mm green pompon
- 2 (¾"-long) twigs
- Low-temperature glue gun

Instructions

1. Cut plastic canvas according to graphs.

2. With pearl cotton, stitch and Overcast pieces following graphs, stitching one mitten cuff with medium emerald green, one with Christmas red and one with garnet. Overcast cuffs with adjacent colors. Work Backstitches and French Knots with 3 strands embroidery floss when stitching and Overcasting are completed.

3. Using photo as a guide through step 7, cut two lengths Christmas red pearl cotton and one length garnet pearl cotton 7"–8" long for hangers. Thread ends of garnet pearl cotton from front to back through holes indicated on teddy bear mitten graph; knot ends.

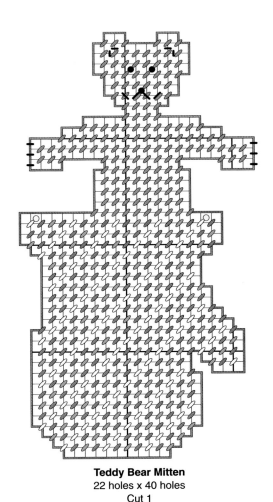

Teddy Bear Mitten
22 holes x 40 holes
Cut 1

COLOR KEY	
DOLL, SNOWMAN & TEDDY BEAR MITTENS	
#3 Pearl Cotton	**Yards**
☐ White	3
■ Christmas red #321	8
▨ Tan brown #436	3
☐ Deep canary #725	1
☐ Pale yellow cream #746	1
▨ Medium topaz #782	1
☐ Pale delft #800	1
▨ Garnet #815	4
▨ Medium blue #826	1
▨ Medium emerald green #911	6
6-Strand Embroidery Floss	
● Black #310 French Knot	1
✔ Black #310 Backstitch	
✐ Bright pumpkin #970 Backstitch	⅙
○ Attach hanger	
Color numbers given are for DMC #3 pearl cotton and 6-strand embroidery floss.	

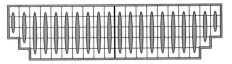

Doll, Snowman & Teddy Bear Mitten Cuff
20 holes x 5 holes
Cut 3
Stitch 1 as graphed,
1 with Christmas red
and 1 with garnet

Repeat with doll and snowman mittens using one length Christmas red for each.

4. Glue corresponding cuffs to mittens.

5. For doll mitten, wrap green ribbon around waist; glue ends to backside. Make a small bow with green ribbon and glue to hair.

6 For teddy bear mitten, make a small bow with burgundy ribbon and glue beneath chin at neckline.

7. For snowman mitten, glue cap to top of head, then glue green pompon to center top of cap. Glue twigs to backside of snowman to resemble arms.

Designed by Celia Lange Designs

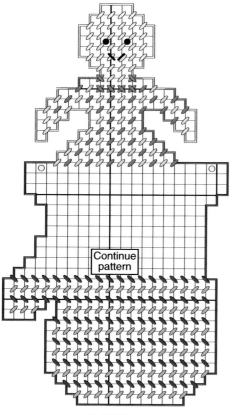

Doll Mitten
21 holes x 38 holes
Cut 1

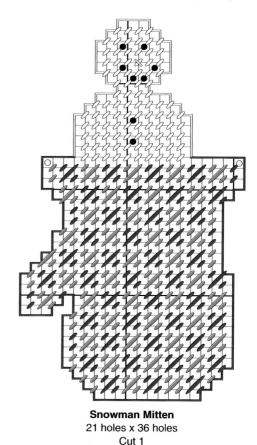

Snowman Mitten
21 holes x 36 holes
Cut 1

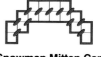

Snowman Mitten Cap
8 holes x 4 holes
Cut 1

COLOR KEY
DOLL, SNOWMAN & TEDDY BEAR MITTENS

#3 Pearl Cotton	Yards
☐ White	3
■ Christmas red #321	8
■ Tan brown #436	3
☐ Deep canary #725	1
☐ Pale yellow cream #746	1
■ Medium topaz #782	1
☐ Pale delft #800	1
■ Garnet #815	4
■ Medium blue #826	1
■ Medium emerald green #911	6

6-Strand Embroidery Floss

● Black #310 French Knot	1
╱ Black #310 Backstitch	
╱ Bright pumpkin #970 Backstitch	⅙
○ Attach hanger	

Color numbers given are for DMC #3 pearl cotton and 6-strand embroidery floss.

Quilt Block Ornament

An embroidered Christmas tree nestled in the center of a colorful quilt block gives this appealing ornament a folk-art look.

Skill Level
Intermediate

Materials
- Small amount 10-count plastic canvas
- DMC #3 pearl cotton as listed in color key
- DMC 6-strand embroidery floss as listed in color key

Instructions

1. Cut plastic canvas according to graph.

2. Stitch piece following graph. Overcast with pale yellow cream. When background stitching and Overcasting are completed, work pearl cotton embroidery over pale yellow cream Reverse Continental Stitches. Backstitch with 3 strands black embroidery floss following graph.

3. For hanger, thread an 8" length of medium dark topaz through hole indicated on graph. Tie ends in a knot to form a loop.

Designed by Celia Lange Designs

COLOR KEY	
#3 Pearl Cotton	**Yards**
☐ Medium dark topaz #783	2
■ Garnet #815	3
◼ Dark antique blue #930	2
◻ Dark willow green #3345	3
Uncoded areas are pale yellow cream #746 Reverse Continental Stitches	2
╱ Pale yellow cream #746 Overcasting	
╱ Medium dark topaz #783 Backstitch	
╱ Dark willow green #3345 Backstitch	
● Garnet #815 French Knot	
6-Strand Embroidery Floss	
╱ Black #310 Backstitch	2
○ Attach hanger	
Color numbers given are for DMC #3 pearl cotton and 6-strand embroidery floss.	

Quilt Block
29 holes x 29 holes
Cut 1

Icicle Santas

Capture Santa's many different faces with this set of sparkling ornaments. Hang them together as a group or scatter them among your tree's other ornaments.

Skill Level

Intermediate

Materials

- 1 sheet 7-count plastic canvas
- Spinrite plastic canvas yarn as listed in color key
- Rhode Island Textile RibbonFloss as listed in color key
- 8 (4mm) dark sapphire round cabochons by The Beadery
- 32" fine silver braid
- Low-temperature glue gun

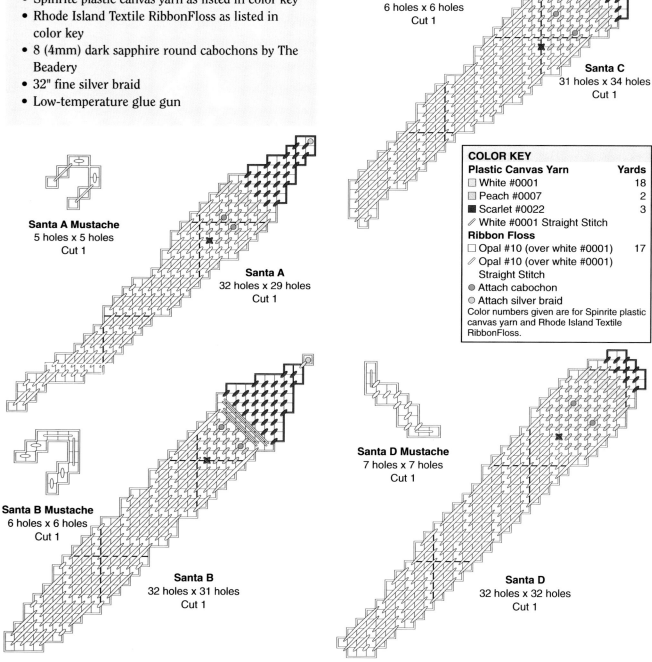

Santa C Mustache
6 holes x 6 holes
Cut 1

Santa C
31 holes x 34 holes
Cut 1

Santa A Mustache
5 holes x 5 holes
Cut 1

Santa A
32 holes x 29 holes
Cut 1

Santa B Mustache
6 holes x 6 holes
Cut 1

Santa B
32 holes x 31 holes
Cut 1

Santa D Mustache
7 holes x 7 holes
Cut 1

Santa D
32 holes x 32 holes
Cut 1

COLOR KEY

Plastic Canvas Yarn	Yards
☐ White #0001	18
☐ Peach #0007	2
■ Scarlet #0022	3
╱ White #0001 Straight Stitch	
Ribbon Floss	
☐ Opal #10 (over white #0001)	17
╱ Opal #10 (over white #0001) Straight Stitch	
● Attach cabochon	
○ Attach silver braid	

Color numbers given are for Spinrite plastic canvas yarn and Rhode Island Textile RibbonFloss.

Instructions

1. Cut plastic canvas according to graphs.

2. Stitch pieces following graphs. Work mustaches and beards with white yarn first, then work ribbon floss over yarn following same pattern.

3. Overcast edges following graphs. Beards and mustaches should be Overcast with yarn first, then with ribbon floss.

4. Glue cabochons where indicated on graphs. Using photo as a guide, glue mustaches to corresponding Santas.

5. Cut four 8" lengths silver braid. Thread one length of braid through hole indicated on each Santa graph; tie ends in knot to form loop for hanging.

Designed by Darla Fanton

Treasures for the Tree 13

Santa's Workshop

Take a peek into Santa bear's busy workshop with this fun-to-stitch ornament.

Skill Level
Beginner

Materials
- ⅛ sheet 10-count plastic canvas
- DMC #3 pearl cotton as listed in color key
- DMC #5 pearl cotton as listed in color key
- #18 tapestry needle
- 1½" flocked Santa bear
- Hot-glue gun

Instructions

1. Cut plastic canvas according to graph.

2. Stitch piece following graph, working Backstitches over completed background stitching. Overcast edges following graph.

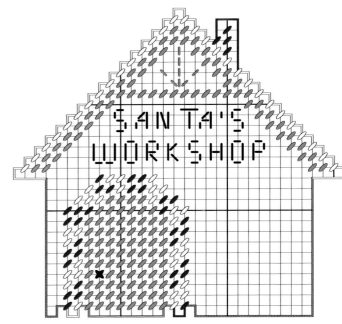

Santa's Workshop
31 holes x 29 holes
Cut 1

COLOR KEY	
#3 Pearl Cotton	**Yards**
☐ White	2
■ Christmas red #321	1
■ Christmas green #909	2
Uncoded areas are tan brown #436 Continental Stitches	5
∕ Tan brown #436 Overcasting	
∕ Christmas green #909 Backstitch	
#5 Pearl Cotton	
■ Black #310	1
∕ Black #310 Backstitch	
Color numbers given are for DMC #3 pearl cotton and DMC #5 pearl cotton.	

3. Glue Santa bear to right of door, making sure bottom edges are even. Cut an 8" length of #3 pearl cotton in desired color and thread through center top of workshop. Tie ends in a knot to form a loop for hanging.

Designed by Angie Arickx

Baby Animals

Baby bunny in her ice skate, baby mice sleeping in their matchbox and baby owl donned with a wreath will steal your heart while adding a sweet touch to your tree! See photo on page 17.

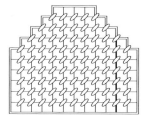

Baby Owl

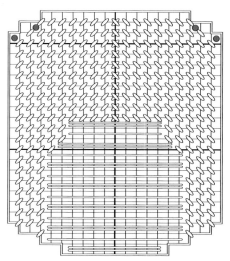

Skill Level
Advanced

Materials
- 1 sheet clear 7-count plastic canvas
- 2 (3") plastic canvas radial circles by Darice
- Spinrite plastic canvas yarn as listed in color key
- 15" Kreinik Fine (#8) Braid: gold #002
- #16 tapestry needle
- 2 (15mm) black round cabochons by The Beadery
- 8 (4mm) ruby round cabochons by The Beadery
- 18" ⅛"-wide red satin ribbon
- Polyester fiberfill
- Hot-glue gun

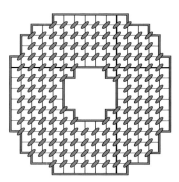

Baby Owl Body Front & Back
20 holes x 23 holes
Stitch front as graphed
Stitch back with white Continental Stitches and
Cross Stitches continuing pattern given

Whipstitch dart
together

Baby Owl Wing Base
7 holes x 11 holes
Cut 2

```
COLOR KEY
BABY OWL
Plastic Canvas Yarn                    Yards
□ White #0001                            28
■ Brisk green #0027                       9
  Clover #0042                            2
□ Mustard #0043                           1
⟋ White #0001 Straight Stitch
● Attach ruby cabochon
Color numbers given are for Spinrite plastic
canvas yarn.
```

Baby Owl Wreath Base
15 holes x 15 holes
Cut 1

Baby Owl Foot
5 holes x 5 holes
Cut 2

Baby Owl Tail Base
12 holes x 10 holes
Cut 1

Back Edge

Baby Owl Beak
5 holes x 4 holes
Cut 2

Baby Owl Feather
5 holes x 6 holes
Cut 14

Baby Owl Holly Leaf
5 holes x 6 holes
Cut 8
Stitch 4 with clover,
4 with brisk green

Instructions

1. Cut plastic canvas according to graphs (page 15). For eyes, cut the first five outer circular threads on each circle so the four innermost circular threads remain.

2. Stitch pieces following graphs. Stitch body front as graphed; stitch body back with white Continental Stitches and Cross Stitches, continuing pattern given. Stitch four holly leaves with brisk green; stitch four with clover.

3. Using white through step 4, Straight Stitch each circle from the first outside row of holes to the third row of holes, using two stitches per hole as necessary in the third row of holes. Overcast circle edge.

4. Whipstitch wrong sides of body front and back together, stuffing firmly with fiberfill before closing. Whipstitch darts of wing bases together with wrong sides facing out. Overcast remaining edges of wing bases.

5. With mustard, Whipstitch beak pieces together along back edges. Overcast all remaining pieces with adjacent colors. Cut four 3" lengths from white. Thread one length through each hole indicated on body graph with a blue dot; tie in a knot and fray ends to resemble feathers.

6. Using photo as a guide through step 9, glue black cabochons to centers of eye circles, then glue eyes to upper body front. Center and glue beak under eyes. Cut a 6" length of ribbon and tie in a bow; trim ends. Glue bow under beak.

7. Glue feet to bottom edge of body at both corners. Following Fig. 1, glue four feathers to wrong side of each wing base. Following Fig. 2, glue six feathers to wrong side of tail base. Glue wings in position on each side of body; center and glue tail to lower back of body.

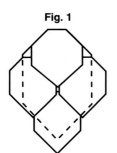

Fig. 1

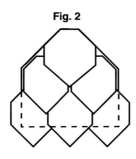

Fig. 2

8. Thread gold braid through center top of owl head; tie ends in a knot to form a loop for hanging.

9. Glue leaves to wrong side of wreath base, alternating colors and overlapping slightly. Glue ruby cabochons to leaves where indicated on graph. Center and glue wreath to top of head, bringing looped hanger through center

hole of wreath. Tie remaining red ribbon in and glue to center back edge of wreath so ribbon tails hang down.

Ice-Skate Bunny

Materials

- 1 sheet clear 7-count plastic canvas
- Spinrite plastic canvas yarn as listed in color key
- Rainbow Gallery Plastic Canvas 7 Metallic Needlepoint Yarn as listed in color key
- 24" Kreinik Heavy (#32) Braid: pearl #032
- 15" Kreinik Fine (#8) Braid: gold #002
- #16 tapestry needle
- 2 (8mm) black round cabochons by The Beadery
- 4mm ruby round cabochon by The Beadery
- ½" white pompon
- 12" ¼"-wide red satin ribbon
- Polyester fiberfill
- Hot-glue gun

Instructions

1. Cut plastic canvas according to graphs (page 18).

2. Stitch pieces following graphs, reversing one skate before stitching. Use 2 plies cherry blossom to stitch nose.

3. Whipstitch wrong sides of head together with silver gray, stuffing with fiberfill before closing. Overcast top edges of skates with white. Whipstitch wrong sides of skates together with adjacent colors, leaving top open. Stuff skate firmly with fiberfill to within 1" of top edge.

4. Using white throughout, Overcast bottom edges of hat pieces; with wrong sides together, Whipstitch remaining edges. With right sides facing, Whipstitch darts on ears together with cherry blossom; Overcast outside edges with silver gray. Overcast all remaining pieces with adjacent colors.

5. Using 2 plies cherry blossom, add Straight Stitches to muzzle and paws.

6. Using photo as a guide through step 8, glue muzzle to face, then glue nose to face and muzzle at center top of muzzle. Glue black cabochons to face above nose. Glue one ear to each side of head.

7. Glue ruby cabochon to leaf where indicated on graph and leaf to front of hat at side. Glue pompon to center top of hat; glue hat to top of head. At green dots on skate, thread and crisscross pearl braid from bottom to

top to resemble lacing; tie in bow at top.

8. Glue head to inside top of skate, then glue paws to top front of skate at each corner. Tie ¼"-wide ribbon around neck, cutting ends to resemble fringe on scarf. Glue ribbon tails to back and front of skate.

9. Thread gold braid through left top hole of hat; tie ends in a knot to form a loop for hanging.

Matchbox Mice

Materials

- 1 sheet clear 7-count plastic canvas
- Spinrite plastic canvas yarn as listed in color key
- 15" Kreinik Fine (#8) Braid: gold #002
- #16 tapestry needle
- 4mm black round cabochon by The Beadery
- 6 (4mm) ruby round cabochons by The Beadery
- 12" ⅛"-wide red satin ribbon
- 12" ⅛"-wide green satin ribbon
- Polyester fiberfill
- Hot-glue gun

Instructions

1. Cut plastic canvas according to graphs (page 18). Cut one 21-hole x 33-hole piece for matchbox bottom and one 20-hole x 16-hole piece for pillow.

2. Stitch pieces following graphs. Stitch four ears with cherry blossom and four with silver gray. Stitch bottom and pillow with white Continental Stitches. Stitch one matchbox short side as graphed; stitch remaining matchbox short side entirely with white Continental Stitches.

3. With 2 plies brisk green, Backstitch letters on matchbox long sides over completed background stitching.

4. Overcast muzzles and paws with silver gray, quilt and pillow with white and leaves with brisk green.

5. Using 2 plies cherry blossom, add Straight Stitches to muzzles and paws and French Knots to muzzles. Stitch one mouse head with two eyes as shown and one with mouse's left eye only. Do not embroider remaining two heads.

6. Whipstitch wrong side of one embroidered head to wrong side of one head without embroidery together with silver gray, stuffing firmly with fiberfill before closing. Repeat with remaining head pieces.

Instructions continued on page 21

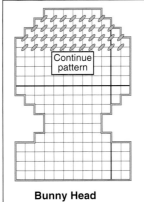

Bunny Head
12 holes x 18 holes
Cut 2

Whipstitch dart together

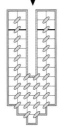

Bunny Ear
5 holes x 12 holes
Cut 2

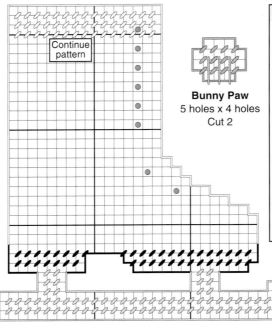

Continue pattern

Continue pattern

Bunny Paw
5 holes x 4 holes
Cut 2

Ice Skate
32 holes x 33 holes
Cut 2, reverse 1

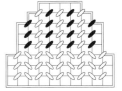

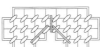

Bunny Muzzle
9 holes x 4 holes
Cut 1

Bunny Nose
3 holes x 2 holes
Cut 1

Bunny Holly Leaf
3 holes x 4 holes
Cut 1

Bunny Hat
10 holes x 8 holes
Cut 2

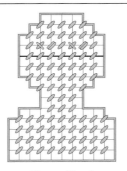

Mouse Head
10 holes x 14 holes
Cut 4

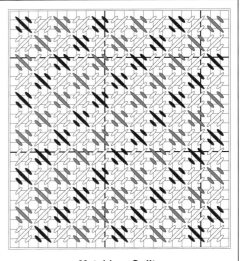

Matchbox Quilt
23 holes x 25 holes
Cut 1

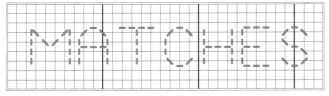

Matchbox Long Side
33 holes x 9 holes
Cut 2

Mouse Ear
4 holes x 4 holes
Cut 8
Stitch 4 as graphed
Stitch 4 with silver gray

Mouse Paw
4 holes x 3 holes
Cut 4

Mouse Muzzle
3 holes x 4 holes
Cut 2

Matchbox Holly Leaf
7 holes x 10 holes
Cut 2

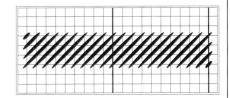

Matchbox Short Side
21 holes x 9 holes
Cut 2

Snowman Family

Stitch each family member's initials on the bottom of these friendly snowmen to give your Christmas tree a personal touch! See photo on page 20.

Skill Level
Beginner

Materials
- 1 sheet 7-count plastic canvas
- Darice Nylon Plus plastic canvas yarn as listed in color key
- DMC 6-strand embroidery floss as listed in color key
- ⅔ yard white #3 pearl cotton
- 10 black giant seed beads by Darice
- White embroidery floss or sewing thread
- Scrap ⅛"-wide dusty rose satin ribbon
- Scrap ⅛"-wide green satin ribbon
- 2 (6mm) gold jingle bells
- 2 (6mm) white pompons
- 8 small twigs
- Low-temperature glue gun

Instructions

1. Cut plastic canvas according to graphs (at right and page 21).

2. Continental Stitch head and body pieces with white, and hat pieces following graphs. Using 6 strands floss throughout, add embroidery to heads following graphs. Using alphabets given, center and Backstitch desired initials in blue shaded area on lower graph bodies. Overcast each piece with yarn following graphs.

3. Add seed beads with white embroidery floss or sewing thread to upper bodies where indicated on graphs. Glue one white pompon each on the daughter's and son's hat tips.

4. Cut four 6" lengths of white pearl cotton. Thread one end through yarn on back of head. Tie ends in a knot to form a loop for hanging.

5. Following photo through step 7, tie dusty rose ribbon in a small bow; glue to Mother's hat. Glue one bell to center bottom of bow.

6. Wrap green ribbon around crown of Father's hat, glue in place, trimming excess ribbon. Tie remaining ribbon in a bow and glue to hat. Glue remaining bell to center bottom of bow.

7. Glue corresponding bodies together by placing upper body on lower body, overlapping two holes. Place head on upper body, overlapping two holes. Glue corresponding hats to heads. For arms, glue twigs to backsides of upper bodies.

Designed by Celia Lange Designs

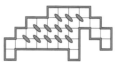

Son Cap
10 holes x 5 holes
Cut 1

Son Head
7 holes x 7 holes
Cut 1

Daughter Head
7 holes x 7 holes
Cut 1

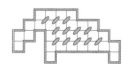

Daughter Cap
10 holes x 5 holes
Cut 1

Daughter & Son Upper Body
8 holes x 8 holes
Cut 2

Daughter & Son Lower Body
10 holes x 10 holes
Cut 2

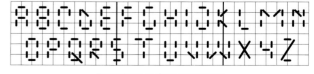

Daughter & Son Alphabet

COLOR KEY	
Plastic Canvas Yarn	**Yards**
■ Black #02	1
☐ Dusty rose #12	1
▨ Holly green #31	1
▦ Violet red #49	1
Uncoded areas are white #01	
Continental Stitches	20
⁄ White #01 Overcasting	
6-Strand Embroidery Floss	
⁄ Black #310 Backstitch	1
⁄ Bright pumpkin #970 Backstitch	¼
● Black #310 French Knot	
● Bright pumpkin #970 French Knot	
● Attach seed beads	

Color numbers given are for Darice Nylon Plus plastic canvas yarn and DMC 6-strand embroidery floss.

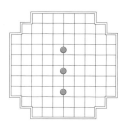

Mother & Father Lower Body
13 holes x 13 holes
Cut 2

Mother & Father Upper Body
10 holes x 10 holes
Cut 2

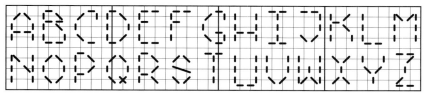

Mother & Father Alphabet

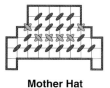

Mother Hat
9 holes x 6 holes
Cut 1

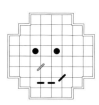

Mother Head
8 holes x 8 holes
Cut 1

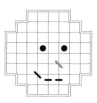

Father Head
8 holes x 8 holes
Cut 1

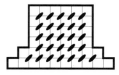

Father Hat
10 holes x 6 holes
Cut 1

Baby Animals

Continued from page 17

7. Whipstitch wrong side of one cherry blossom ear and wrong side of one silver gray ear together with silver gray. Repeat with remaining ear pieces.

8. Using white throughout, Overcast top edges of matchbox sides. Whipstitch sides together, then sides to bottom.

Assembly

1. Tie one ribbon in a small bow around each mouse neck, trimming ends as desired. Glue black cabochon for remaining eye to mouse with one stitched eye. Glue pillow at an angle in matchbox to one short side and to bottom.

2. Using photo as a guide throughout, glue ears to corners of heads with cherry blossom sides facing front. Glue heads to pillow. With top edge of quilt near mice shoulders, glue quilt to top edges of matchbox. Glue paws to top edge of quilt.

3. Glue ruby cabochons to leaves where indicated on graph. Glue leaves at an angle to short side stitched entirely with white so that bottoms of leaves are in the middle and points are in upper corners.

4. Thread gold braid through one corner of matchbox bed; tie ends in a knot to form a loop for hanging.

Designed by Vicki Blizzard

Peppermint Candy Bluebird

You'll find yourself smiling with every stitch as you create this charming bluebird ornament. His warmth is infectious, so be sure to share him with family and friends!

Skill Level
Intermediate

Materials
- ½ sheet 7-count plastic canvas
- 4 (3") plastic canvas radial circles
- Spinrite plastic canvas yarn as listed in color key
- #16 tapestry needle
- 2 (8mm) black round cabochons by The Beadery
- ½" green pompon
- 6" ¼"-wide green satin ribbon
- 11" Kreinik Fine (#8) Braid: gold #002HL
- Craft glue
- Hot-glue gun

Cutting & Stitching
1. Cut plastic canvas according to graphs. For head, cut the first two outermost rows of holes from two radial circles. Do not trim any rows from two remaining body circles.

2. Stitch pieces following graphs, reversing two wings before stitching. One beak piece will remain unstitched. With 2 plies brisk green, work French Knots on hat pieces.

3. With white, Overcast bottom edges of hat pieces, then Whipstitch wrong sides of hat pieces together along sides and top. Overcast feet with daffodil and cheeks with cherry blossom.

4. Using white through step 5, Cross Stitch across center row of holes on each body circle. Straight Stitch from the center row of holes to the third row of holes, using four stitches per hole in each center hole.

5. Continuing outward, Straight Stitch around circle from the third row of holes to the fifth row, using two stitches per hole as necessary in the third row of holes. Repeat one more time from the fifth row of holes to the seventh.

6. With scarlet and white, Straight Stitch from the seventh row of holes to the outermost row of holes, alternating colors.

7. Using royal through step 8, Cross Stitch across cen-

Fig. 1

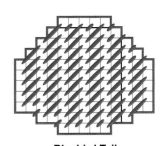

COLOR KEY

Plastic Canvas Yarn	Yards
☐ White #0001	13
☐ Cherry blossom #0010	2
■ Scarlet #0022	13
■ Royal #0026	28
☐ Daffodil #0029	3
● Brisk green #0027 French Knot	1
● Attach gold braid	

Color numbers given are for Spinrite plastic canvas yarn.

Bluebird Tail
13 holes x 11 holes
Cut 2

Bluebird Heart
7 holes x 7 holes
Cut 4

Bluebird Cheek
4 holes x 4 holes
Cut 2

ter row of holes on each head circle. Straight Stitch from the center row of holes to the third row of holes, using four stitches per hole in each center hole.

8. Continuing outward, Straight Stitch around circle from the third row of holes to the fifth row, using two stitches per hole as necessary in the third row of holes. Repeat one more time from the fifth row of holes to the outermost row of holes.

Assembly

1. Whipstitch wrong sides of body pieces together with scarlet and white, alternating colors. Using royal through step 2, Overcast 13 holes on both head circles. With wrong sides together and 13 holes of each piece back to back, Whipstitch remaining edges of head pieces together.

2. Matching edges, Whipstitch wrong sides of two wing pieces together. Repeat with remaining two wing pieces. Whipstitch wrong sides of tail pieces together.

3. Whipstitch two heart pieces together with scarlet. Repeat with remaining two heart pieces. Cut a 5¼" length of gold braid. Tie one heart to each end of braid where indicated on graph; secure knots with a dot of craft glue.

4. Using daffodil throughout, Overcast two edges of one stitched beak from dot to dot. Repeat with second stitched beak. Whipstitch remaining two edges of one stitched beak to two edges of unstitched beak. Repeat with second stitched beak and remaining edges of unstitched beak. Bend and mold beak so unstitched back lies flat enough to glue. Open beak and insert center of gold braid with hearts on each end; glue braid in beak with craft glue.

5. Following photo and Fig. 1 through step 6, hot-glue beak, cheeks and cabochons for eyes to face. Thread remaining gold braid through center top of hat; tie ends in a knot to form a loop for hanging. Glue green pompon to center top of hat and front of braid. Insert head in opening of hat and glue in place.

6. Insert body in opening of head and glue in place. Glue wings and tail to back of body. Glue feet to front of body.

Designed by Vicki Blizzard

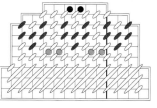

Bluebird Hat
14 holes x 9 holes
Cut 2

Bluebird Beak
4 holes x 4 holes
Cut 3, stitch 2

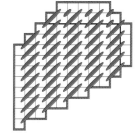

Bluebird Wing
11 holes x 12 holes
Cut 4, reverse 2

Bluebird Foot
5 holes x 7 holes
Cut 2

Country Baskets

Filled with chocolates, candy canes or tiny gifts,
these pleasing ornaments are a double delight!

Skill Level
Beginner

Materials
- 1 sheet 7-count plastic canvas
- Small amount 10-count plastic canvas
- Darice Nylon Plus plastic canvas yarn as listed in color key
- DMC #3 pearl cotton as listed in color key
- 6" each ¼"-wide satin ribbon: burgundy, gold, cream and dark green
- Low-temperature glue gun

Instructions

1. Cut basket fronts and backs, sides and handles from 7-count plastic canvas; cut goose, house, heart and pineapple motifs from 10-count plastic canvas according to graphs.

2. For basket, with yarn, stitch one front and back, one side and one handle following graphs. Stitch one set of basket pieces replacing white with baby yellow and baby yellow with gold; stitch one set replacing white with holly green and baby yellow with forest green and one set replacing white with dusty rose and baby yellow with violet.

3. Using the darker color of each set, Overcast handles, top edges of basket fronts and backs and short edges of sides. Whipstitch long edges of sides to front and back pieces. Glue basket handles to outside edges of sides, overlapping three holes.

4. Stitch motifs with #3 pearl cotton following graphs. Overcast pieces following graphs. Work ultra dark pistachio green Backstitches and Straight Stitch when background stitching and Overcasting are completed.

5. Glue motifs to center basket fronts as follows: house

to white and baby yellow basket, heart to baby yellow and gold basket, goose to holly green and forest green basket, and pineapple to dusty rose and violet basket.

6. Tie each length of ribbon into a bow, trimming tails as desired. Glue to front top corners of basket as follows: gold bow to white and baby yellow basket, dark green bow to yellow and gold basket, burgundy bow to holly green and forest green basket, and cream bow to dusty rose and violet basket.

Designed by Celia Lange Designs

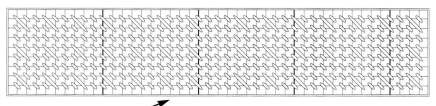

Basket Side
44 holes x 9 holes
Cut 4 from 7-count
Stitch 1 with yarn as graphed
Stitch 1 replacing white with baby yellow
and baby yellow with gold
Stitch 1 replacing white with holly green
and baby yellow with forest green
Stitch 1 replacing white with dusty rose
and baby yellow with violet

Basket Handle
42 holes x 3 holes
Cut 4 from 7-count
Stitch 1 with yarn as graphed
Stitch 1 replacing white with baby yellow
and baby yellow with gold
Stitch 1 replacing white with holly green
and baby yellow with forest green
Stitch 1 replacing white with dusty rose
and baby yellow with violet

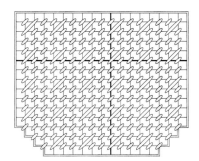

Basket Front & Back
18 holes x 15 holes
Cut 8 from 7-count
Stitch 2 with yarn as graphed
Stitch 2 replacing white with baby
yellow and baby yellow with gold
Stitch 2 replacing white with holly green
and baby yellow with forest green
Stitch 2 replacing white with dusty rose
and baby yellow with violet

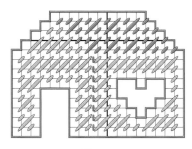

House
18 holes x 13 holes
Cut 1 from 10-count
Stitch with pearl cotton

COLOR KEY	
Plastic Canvas Yarn	**Yards**
☐ White #01	6
Dusty rose #12	6
Gold #27	13
Holly green #31	6
Forest green #32	13
☐ Baby yellow #42	19
Violet #49	13
#3 Pearl Cotton	
☐ White	3
▨ Medium shell pink #223	2
▨ Golden mustard #832	3
▨ Ultra dark pistachio green #890	4
■ Very dark garnet #902	3
▨ Willow green #904	5
╱ Ultra dark pistachio green #890 Backstitch and Straight Stitch	
Color numbers given are for Darice Nylon Plus plastic canvas yarn and DMC #3 pearl cotton.	

Pineapple
11 holes x 20 holes
Cut 1 from 10-count
Stitch with pearl cotton

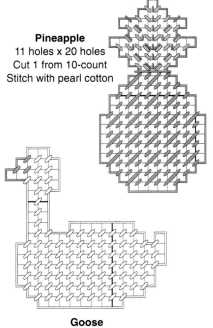

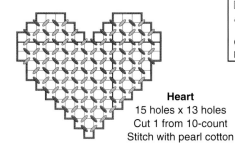

Heart
15 holes x 13 holes
Cut 1 from 10-count
Stitch with pearl cotton

Goose
15 holes x 15 holes
Cut 1 from 10-count
Stitch with pearl cotton

Mini Toys

Instructions begin on page 31

Gifts For All

Festive Gift Boxes
Instructions begin on page 28

Festive Gift Boxes

Give two charming gifts at the same time by using either of these country gift boxes instead of wrapping paper!

See photo on pages 26 and 27.

Christmas Goose

Skill Level
Beginner

Materials
- 1½ sheets 7-count plastic canvas
- Uniek Needloft plastic canvas yarn as listed in color key
- DMC #3 pearl cotton as listed in color key
- Small bunch silk holly with berries
- Hot-glue gun

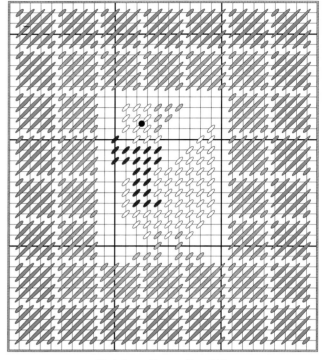

Christmas Goose Box Side
29 holes x 33 holes
Cut 4

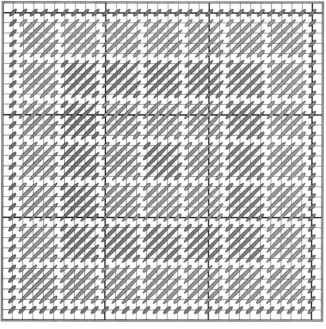

Christmas Goose Lid Top
31 holes x 31 holes
Cut 1

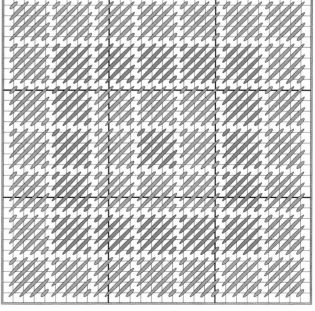

Christmas Goose Box Bottom
29 holes x 29 holes
Cut 1

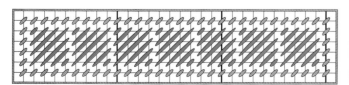

Christmas Goose Lid Side
31 holes x 7 holes
Cut 4

COLOR KEY
CHRISTMAS GOOSE

Plastic Canvas Yarn	Yards
■ Red #01	3
▨ Rose #06	50
▢ Tangerine #11	3
▨ Holly #27	50
□ White #41	7
Uncoded areas are cerulean #34 Continental Stitches	8

#3 Pearl Cotton
● Black French Knot	1

Color numbers given are for Uniek Needloft plastic canvas yarn.

Instructions

1. Cut plastic canvas according to graphs.

2. Stitch pieces following graphs. Add black pearl cotton French Knot when background stitching is completed.

3. Using rose throughout, Overcast bottom edges of lid sides and top edges of box sides. Whipstitch box sides together, then Whipstitch sides to bottom. Whipstitch lid sides together, then Whipstitch lid sides to lid top.

4. Center and glue holly to lid top.

Noel

Skill Level
Beginner

Materials
- 2 sheets 7-count plastic canvas
- Uniek Needloft plastic canvas yarn as listed in color key
- Small amount silk holly leaves and berries
- Miniature red cardinal
- Hot-glue gun

Instructions

1. Cut and stitch plastic canvas according to graphs (below and page 30).

2. Using white throughout, Overcast bottom edges of lid sides and top edges of box sides. Whipstitch lid sides together, then Whipstitch lid sides to lid top. Whipstitch box sides together, then Whipstitch box sides to box bottom.

3. Center and glue holly leaves and berries to lid top. Glue cardinal in leaves.

Designed by Michele Wilcox

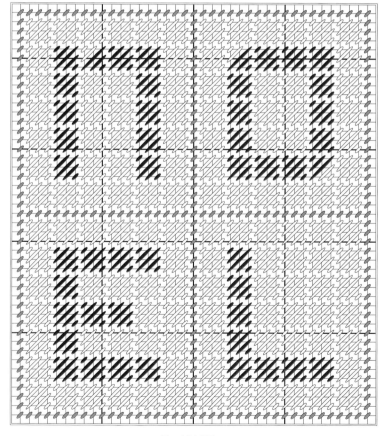

Noel Lid Top
40 holes x 46 holes
Cut 1

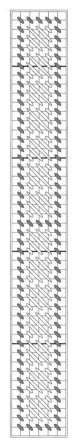

Noel Lid Long Side
6 holes x 46 holes
Cut 2

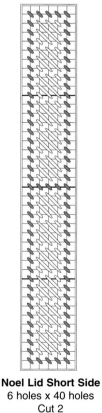

Noel Lid Short Side
6 holes x 40 holes
Cut 2

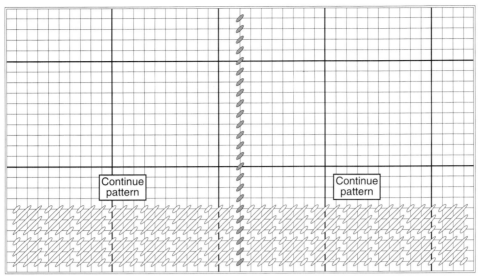

Noel Box Long Side
44 holes x 25 holes
Cut 2

COLOR KEY
NOEL

Plastic Canvas Yarn	Yards
■ Red #01	6
▨ Holly #27	8
☐ White #41	100

Color numbers given are for Uniek Needloft plastic canvas yarn.

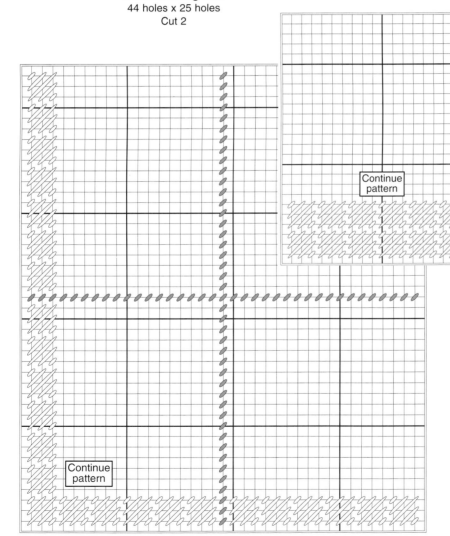

Noel Box Short Side
38 holes x 25 holes
Cut 2

Noel Box Bottom
38 holes x 44 holes
Cut 1

Mini Toys

Delight a little boy with these colorful toys tucked into his Christmas stocking. They're perfect for playtime, and make colorful shelf decorations, too. See photo on pages 26 and 27.

Drum Box

Skill Level
Beginner

Materials
- ⅓ sheet 7-count clear plastic canvas
- Small amount 7-count beige plastic canvas
- 2 (3") plastic canvas radial circles by Darice
- Coats & Clark Red Heart Classic Art. E267 worsted weight yarn as listed in color key
- Westrim Crafts white Fun Foam
- 6" ⅛"-wide red satin ribbon
- Hot-glue gun

Cutting & Stitching

1. Cut lid band, base band and drum side from clear plastic canvas; cut drumsticks from beige plastic canvas according to graphs.

2. On both radial circles, cut away the five outermost rows of holes so that only the eight innermost rows of holes remain. Using one circle as a template, cut one piece white craft foam slightly smaller than circle.

3. Stitch bands and side following graphs. Do not add honey gold Straight Stitches to side at this time. Backstitch drumsticks with honey gold. Do not Overcast drumsticks.

4. Using off-white through step 6, Straight Stitch each circle from the first outside row of holes to the fourth outside row of holes, using two stitches per hole as necessary in the fourth row of holes.

5. Moving toward the center, Straight Stitch around circle from the fourth row of holes to the sixth row of holes, using two stitches per hole in the sixth row of holes as necessary.

6. Repeat one more time from the sixth row of holes to the center row. Work Cross Stitch in the center.

7. With country red, Overcast top and bottom edges of side; Whipstitch short edges together. Straight Stitch side with honey gold.

Assembly

1. Using paddy green through step 3, Overcast bottom edge of lid band; Whipstitch short edges together. Overcast top edge of base band; Whipstitch short edges together.

2. Whipstitch one circle to top edge of lid band, forming drum box lid. Whipstitch remaining circle to bottom edge of base band, forming drum base.

3. Glue craft foam circle to inside of drum base. Glue base to bottom edge of side.

4. Forming an "X," center and glue drumsticks to top of drum lid. Thread ends of ribbon from back to front through center holes of circle on both sides of drumsticks. Tie ribbon in a bow and glue to secure. Place lid on box.

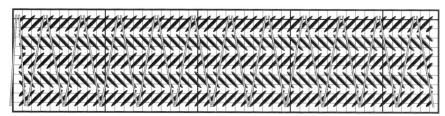

Drum Side
46 holes x 11 holes
Cut 1 from clear

COLOR KEY	
DRUM BOX	
Worsted Weight Yarn	**Yards**
Off-white #03	5
▩ Paddy green #686	7
■ Country red #914	8
⁄ Honey gold #645 Backstitch	3
Color numbers given are for Coats & Clark Red Heart Classic Art. E267 worsted weight yarn.	

Drumstick
18 holes x 1 hole
Cut 2 from beige

Drum Lid Band & Base Band
52 holes x 2 holes
Cut 2 from clear

Sled

Materials
- ¼ sheet 7-count clear plastic canvas
- Small amount 7-count black plastic canvas
- Coats & Clark Red Heart Classic Art. E267 worsted weight yarn as listed in color key
- Hot-glue gun

Instructions

1. Cut sled boards, crossbar and braces from clear plastic canvas; cut sled runners from black plastic canvas according to graphs. Cut out blue lines on sled runner graph, leaving black lines only. Sled runners will remain unstitched.

2. Stitch pieces following graphs. Overcast sled boards, crossbar and braces with warm brown, then work Backstitches and French Knots.

3. Glue braces to backside of sled boards as shown in Fig. 1. Using photo as a guide, glue crossbar across top edges of boards.

4. Glue runners to underside of sled boards and to ends of braces.

5. For hanger, cut a 6" length of country red yarn. Threads ends from front to back through holes indicated on crossbar graph. Knot ends on backside.

Wagon

Materials
- ¼ sheet 7-count clear plastic canvas
- Small amount 7-count black plastic canvas
- 4 (3") plastic canvas radial circles by Darice
- Coats & Clark Red Heart Classic Art. E267 worsted weight yarn as listed in color key
- 2 (2½") lengths ¼"-diameter dowels
- Hot-glue gun

Cutting & Stitching

1. Cut wagon bottom and sides from clear plastic canvas; cut wagon tongue and handle from black plastic canvas according to graphs (page 40).

2. On all four radial circles, cut away all but the three innermost circular threads.

3. Stitch pieces following graphs. Wagon tongue will remain unstitched. Do not Overcast handle.

4. With country red, Overcast top edges of sides; Whipstitch sides together; with right side of bottom facing up, Whipstitch bottom to sides. Work paddy green Backstitches on sides and around corners.

5. For wheels, Straight Stitch circles with yellow from the outermost row of holes to the center row of holes. Cross Stitch with country red at center of circles. Overcast with black.

Assembly

1. With country red, stitch tongue to underside of wagon where indicated with blue dots; for front and rear axles, stitch dowels to underside of wagon where indicated. Glue wheels to ends of axles.

3. Insert smaller end of handle into cutout area of tongue.

Designed by Celia Lange Designs

Fig. 1

Sled Crossbar
18 holes x 4 holes
Cut 1 from clear

Sled Brace
11 holes x 2 holes
Cut 2 from clear

```
COLOR KEY
SLED
Worsted Weight Yarn                          Yards
■ Warm brown #336                              10
⁄ Paddy green #686 Backstitch                   1
⁄ Country red #914 Backstitch                   4
● Country red #914 French Knot
● Attach yarn for hanger
Color numbers given are for Coats & Clark Red
Heart Classic Art. E267 worsted weight yarn.
```

Sled Runner
21 holes x 2 holes
Cut 2 from black
Cut out blue lines,
leaving black lines only
Do not stitch

Sled Side Board
3 holes x 21 holes
Cut 2 from clear

Sled Center Board
4 holes x 23 holes
Cut 1 from clear

Wagon graphs are on page 40

Heart-to-Heart Accessories

Add a country touch to any casual outfit with this coordinating pin and barrette set. Soft pastels worked into pretty hearts make lovely accessories.

Skill Level
Beginner

Materials
- Scraps 10-count plastic canvas
- DMC #3 pearl cotton as listed in color key
- DMC 6-strand embroidery floss as listed in color key
- ⅜" pink heart button
- ½" pink heart button
- Sewing needle and ivory thread
- 1¼" pin back
- 3" barrette back
- Low-temperature glue gun

Instructions

1. Cut four plastic canvas hearts according to graph.

2. Stitch hearts following graph. Overcast with dark willow green pearl cotton. When background stitching and Overcasting are completed, Backstitch with 2 strands dark willow green embroidery floss.

3. With sewing needle and ivory thread, sew large heart button to center of one heart for barrette; for pin, sew small heart button to right side of one heart (see photo).

4. Glue pin back to wrong side of heart with small button. For barrette, glue remaining three hearts together following Fig. 1. Center and glue barrette back to wrong side of barrette.

Designed by Celia Lange Designs

Fig. 1

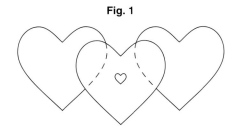

Heart
17 holes x 16 holes
Cut 1 for pin
Cut 3 for barrette

COLOR KEY	
#3 Pearl Cotton	Yards
Medium shell pink #223	5
Light pistachio green #368	5
Pale yellow cream #746	5
Light antique blue #932	5
Dark willow green #3345 Overcasting	4
6-Strand Embroidery Floss	
Dark willow green #3345 Backstitch	2
Color numbers given are for DMC #3 pearl cotton and 6-strand embroidery floss.	

Jolly St. Nick

You'll find many uses for these whimsical Santas. Tie to a package or glue to a purchased basket to add a creative touch to your gift-giving!

Skill Level
Beginner

Materials
- 1½ sheets 7-count plastic canvas
- Spinrite plastic canvas yarn as listed in color key
- Rainbow Gallery Plastic Canvas 7 Metallic Needlepoint Yarn as listed in color key
- #16 tapestry needle
- 3 (1") white pompons
- Hot-glue gun

Instructions

1. Cut plastic canvas according to graph.

2. Stitch pieces following graph, Overcasting edges with adjacent colors while stitching. ***Note:** Face areas are Overcast with white.*

3. Backstitch eyes and line at bottom of jacket with 2 plies black yarn. Wrap scarlet yarn around needle two times for French Knot nose.

4. Glue pompons to tips of caps.

Designed by Joan Green

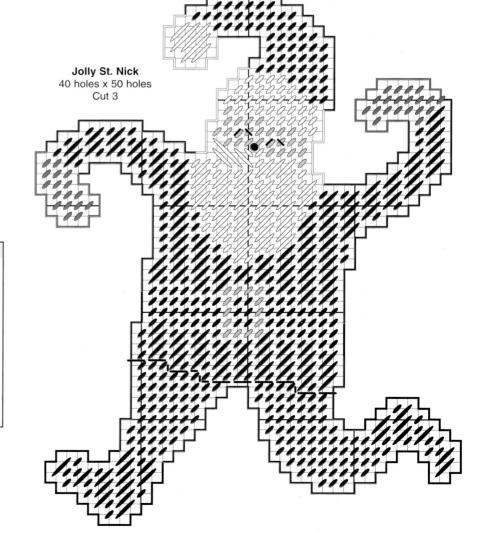

Jolly St. Nick
40 holes x 50 holes
Cut 3

COLOR KEY	
Plastic Canvas Yarn	**Yards**
☐ White #0001	9
▦ Peach #0007	3
■ Scarlet #0022	30
▨ Brisk green #0027	6
■ Black #0028	12
● Scarlet #0022 French Knot	
╱ Black #0028 Backstitch	
1⁄16 " Metallic Needlepoint Yarn	
☐ Gold #PC 1	¾
Color numbers given are for Spinrite plastic canvas yarn and Rainbow Gallery Plastic Canvas 7 Metallic Needlepoint Yarn.	

Home Is Where the Heart Is

This unique tissue box cover borrows two traditional quilt motifs to make a warm accent for any country home!

Skill Level
Beginner

Materials
- 1¼ sheets 7-count plastic canvas
- Uniek Needloft plastic canvas yarn as listed in color key
- #18 tapestry needle
- 6 (⅝") 2-hole white buttons
- Raffia

Instructions
1. Cut plastic canvas according to graphs.

2. Stitch pieces following graphs. Overcast bottom edges of sides with sail blue and inner edges of top with beige.

3. Place buttons where indicated on graphs. Thread needle with raffia; bring needle from front to back through one button hole, then from back to front through remaining hole. Remove needle; tie raffia in a bow. Trim tails as desired.

4. Whipstitch sides together with sail blue and beige following graph. Whipstitch top to sides with sail blue.

Designed by Kathy Wirth

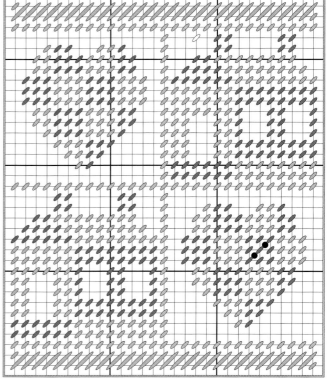

Home Is Where the Heart Is Side
30 holes x 36 holes
Cut 4

COLOR KEY	
Plastic Canvas Yarn	**Yards**
■ Navy #31	35
▨ Sail blue #35	22
▨ Beige #40	15
Uncoded areas are white #41	
Continental Stitches	23
● Attach button	
Color numbers given are for Uniek Needloft plastic canvas yarn.	

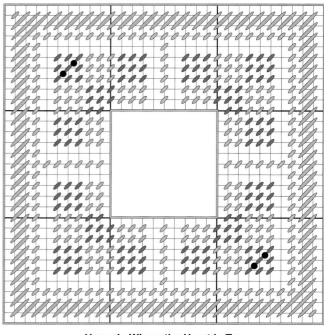

Home Is Where the Heart Is Top
30 holes x 30 holes
Cut 1

Blossoms & Lace

Two easy-to-make projects, a sweet photo frame with heart-shaped cutout and small potpourri basket, make lovely gifts the recipients will use again and again.

Card

Skill Level
Beginner

Materials
- ½ sheet 7-count plastic canvas
- Uniek Needloft plastic canvas yarn as listed in color key
- 10¾" x 7½" piece rose construction paper
- 1 yard off-white lace
- Hot-glue gun

Instructions

1. Cut plastic canvas according to graph (page 40).

2. Stitch card front following graph. Overcast inside and outside edges with lavender.

3. Center and glue photo behind heart opening. Glue lace to backside of card front around outside edge, trimming as necessary.

4. Fold rose construction paper in half so folded measurement is 5⅜" x 7½". Glue card front to front of construction paper. Add message to inside of card as desired.

Gift Basket

Skill Level
Beginner

Materials
- 1 sheet 7-count plastic canvas
- Uniek Needloft plastic canvas yarn as listed in color key
- ½ yard off-white lace
- Hot-glue gun

Instructions

1. Cut plastic canvas according to graphs (at right and page 40).

2. Stitch pieces following graphs. Overcast handle edges with mermaid and top edges of sides with lavender.

3. With lavender, Whipstitch sides together, then Whipstitch bottom to sides.

4. Glue lace around top inside edge of basket, trimming as necessary. Glue handles to outside of basket where indicated on graph.

Designed by Michele Wilcox

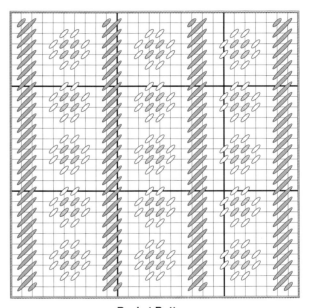

Basket Bottom
27 holes x 27 holes
Cut 1

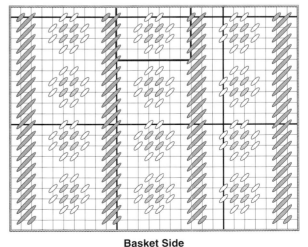

Basket Side
27 holes x 21 holes
Cut 4

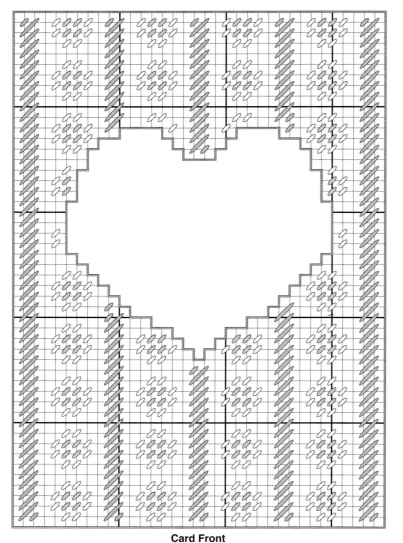

Card Front
35 holes x 49 holes
Cut 1

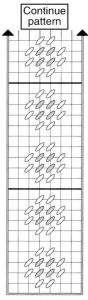

Continue pattern

Basket Handle
7 holes x 90 holes
Cut 1

Mini Toys

Continued from page 32

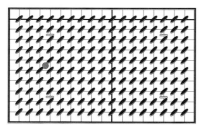

Wagon Bottom
18 holes x 11 holes
Cut 1 from clear

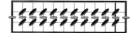

Wagon Short Side
11 holes x 3 holes
Cut 2 from clear

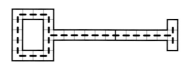

Handle
16 holes x 5 holes
Cut 1 from black

Tongue
7 holes x 2 holes
Cut 1 from black
Do not stitch

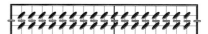

Wagon Long Side
18 holes x 3 holes
Cut 2 from clear

Country Hearts Basket

Colorful button fabric, colored canvas and just a few stitches and you'll have this super-quick gift basket for filling with holiday goodies!

Skill Level
Beginner

Materials
- 2½ sheets country blue 7-count plastic canvas
- Uniek Needloft plastic canvas yarn as listed in color key
- ¼ yard 45"-wide coordinating print fabric (sample used button print)
- Black ultra-fine-point permanent marking pen
- 12 small assorted buttons
- Hot-glue gun

Instructions

1. Cut plastic canvas according to graphs (pages 42 and 43). Cut one 47-hole x 38-hole piece for basket bottom.

2. Following graphs, Continental Stitch hearts on handle and on top edges of basket front, back and sides. Overcast edges of stitched hearts with adjacent colors.

3. From coordinating print fabric cut two 1¼" x 45" strips and two 1½" x 22" strips. Set one of the 1¼" x 45" strips aside; cut remaining 1¼" x 45" strip in half. From remaining fabric, cut two large and four small hearts following patterns given.

4. Using black marking pen and Fig. 1 as a guide, mark around edges of fabric hearts to simulate stitches.

5. Using photo as a guide, glue one large and two small hearts each to basket front and back. Glue four buttons as desired to each large heart and one button to center of each small heart.

6. Using lavender throughout, Whipstitch basket front, back and sides together; Whipstitch bottom to basket. Center handle on back of sides between the two stitched hearts, then Continental Stitch with lavender over previous stitching. ***Note:** Handle will be one hole off center.*

7. Weave 1¼" x 45" fabric strip through slits at top of basket. Begin by coming up through center front slit; end by going down through center front slit. Trim ends and glue to fabric on backside of basket front.

8. Tie four bows with remaining fabric strips. Using photo as a guide, glue one bow to center top of each basket side under heart top border. Trim tails to desired length.

Designed by Louise Arganbright

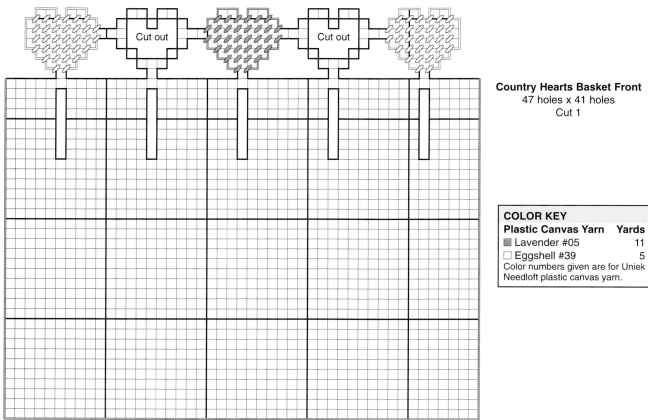

Country Hearts Basket Front
47 holes x 41 holes
Cut 1

COLOR KEY

Plastic Canvas Yarn	Yards
▨ Lavender #05	11
☐ Eggshell #39	5

Color numbers given are for Uniek
Needloft plastic canvas yarn.

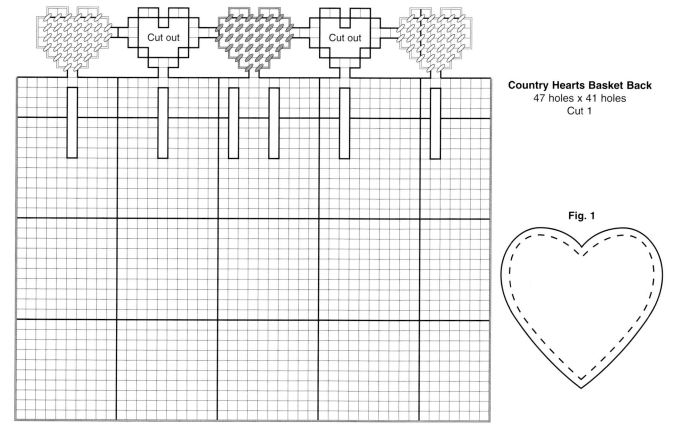

Country Hearts Basket Back
47 holes x 41 holes
Cut 1

Fig. 1

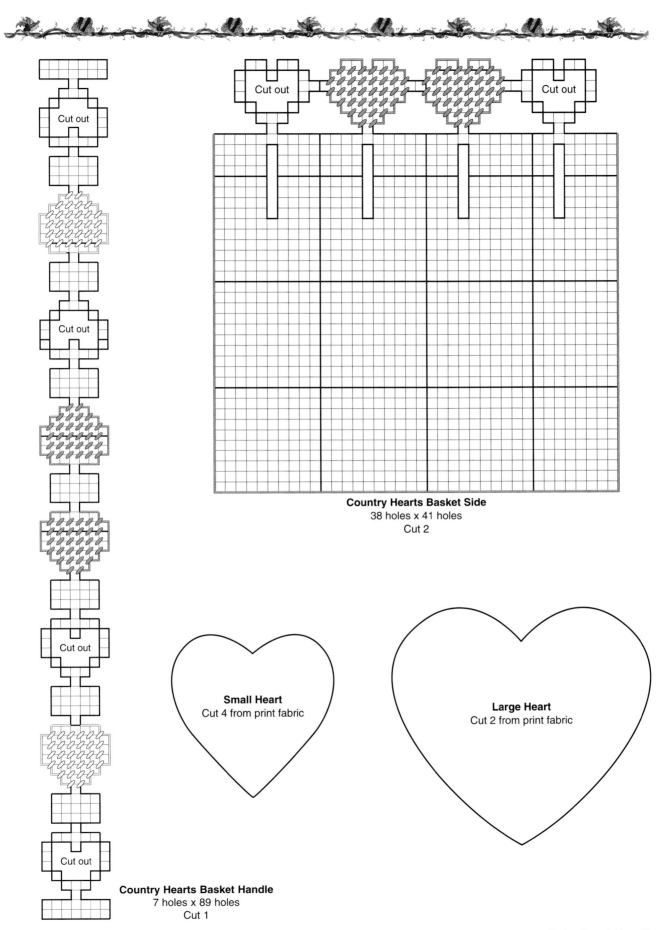

Country Hearts Basket Side
38 holes x 41 holes
Cut 2

Small Heart
Cut 4 from print fabric

Large Heart
Cut 2 from print fabric

Country Hearts Basket Handle
7 holes x 89 holes
Cut 1

Pet Goodie Keepers

Filled with doggie biscuits or kitty treats, your furry friends will surely thank you for these Christmas gifts!

Skill Level
Intermediate

Materials
- 1 sheet Uniek Quick-Count 7-count plastic canvas
- Uniek Needloft plastic canvas yarn as listed in color key
- 8" Uniek Needloft Craft Cord: green #04
- 2 (1-quart) plastic jars with plastic lids by The New Berlin Co.
- 2 (10mm) gold jingle bells
- Craft and fabric glue

Cutting & Stitching

1. Cut plastic canvas according to graphs (also see page 46).

2. Stitch pieces following graphs, reversing one cat ear before stitching. Stitch one bow with Christmas red for cat. Stitch remaining bow with Christmas green for dog. Backstitch around eyes over completed Continental Stitching.

3. Overcast bottom edge of cat collar with Christmas red and bottom edge of dog collar with Christmas green. Overcast noses, top and bottom edges of bows and side and bottom edges of tongues with adjacent colors.

4. Overcast side and top edges of cat ears with gray. Overcast side edges of dog ears with white. Overcast side and bottom edges of dog ear tips with black.

Assembly

1. With Christmas red, Whipstitch top edges of tongues to heads where indicated on graphs. With pink, tack cat nose to cat muzzle where indicated on graphs. With black, tack dog nose to dog muzzle where indicated on graphs.

2. For whiskers, cut green plastic canvas metallic cord in half. On left side of cat's nose, thread ends of one length from back to front through holes indicated on graph. Repeat with remaining length on right side of nose. Dab a small amount of glue on cord ends to keep them from fraying.

3. With white, Whipstitch top edge of cat muzzle spacer to cat head where indicated on graph. With gray,

Overcast bottom edge of cat muzzle, then Whipstitch bottom edge of spacer to side and top edges of cat muzzle.

4. With gray, Whipstitch top edge of dog muzzle spacer to dog head where indicated on graph. With white, Overcast bottom edge of dog muzzle, then Whipstitch bottom edge of spacer to side and top edges of dog muzzle.

5. Making sure seam of collar is at top edge of cat head, Whipstitch top edges of cat collar to cat head with white, Whipstitching ears in place at dots while attaching collar to head.

6. Repeat step 5 with dog collar, head and ears, Whipstitching together with gray. With wrong side of dog left ear tip on right side of dog left ear, Whipstitch top edge of ear to top edge of ear tip with black. Repeat with right dog ear pieces.

7. With wrong sides together, tack edges of bows to center fronts of bows with adjacent colors.

8. With Christmas red, tack cat bow to top center of cat collar under tongue by wrapping yarn around center of bow several times. Add jingle bell on last stitch around bow (see photo). Repeat for dog bow using Christmas green yarn.

9. Fill jars as desired. Slide stitched cat and dog on plastic jars.

Designed by Mary T. Cosgrove

COLOR KEY	
Plastic Canvas Yarn	**Yards**
■ Black #00	4
■ Christmas red #02	13
□ Pink #07	3
▨ Christmas green #28	12
▨ Gray #38	14
□ White #41	15
Uncoded area on dog head is gray #38 Continental Stitches	
Uncoded area on cat head is white #41 Continental Stitches	
╱ Black #00 Backstitch	
╱ Christmas green #28 Backstitch	
╱ Attach tongue	
╱ Attach nose to muzzle	
● Attach cat whiskers	
╱ Attach muzzle spacer	
Color numbers given are for Uniek Needloft plastic canvas yarn.	

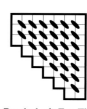

Dog's Left Ear Tip
7 holes x 8 holes
Cut 1

Dog's Right Ear Tip
7 holes x 8 holes
Cut 1

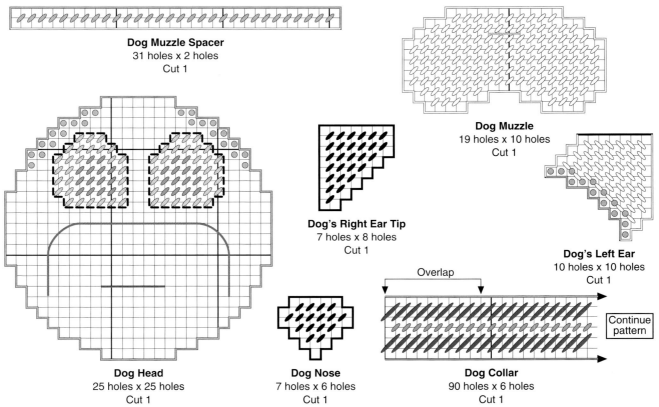

Dog Muzzle Spacer
31 holes x 2 holes
Cut 1

Dog Muzzle
19 holes x 10 holes
Cut 1

Dog's Right Ear Tip
7 holes x 8 holes
Cut 1

Dog's Left Ear
10 holes x 10 holes
Cut 1

Dog Head
25 holes x 25 holes
Cut 1

Dog Nose
7 holes x 6 holes
Cut 1

Overlap

Continue pattern

Dog Collar
90 holes x 6 holes
Cut 1

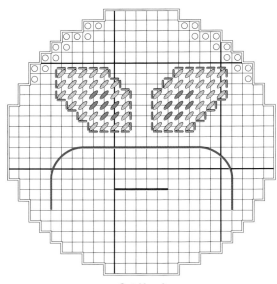

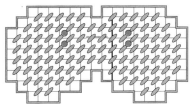

Cat Muzzle
17 holes x 9 holes
Cut 1

Cat Head
25 holes x 25 holes
Cut 1

Cat Nose
5 holes x 3 holes
Cut 1

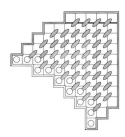

Cat Ear
10 holes x 11 holes
Cut 2, reverse 1

COLOR KEY	
Plastic Canvas Yarn	**Yards**
■ Black #00	4
■ Christmas red #02	13
□ Pink #07	3
■ Christmas green #28	12
■ Gray #38	14
□ White #41	15

Uncoded area on dog head is
gray #38 Continental Stitches
Uncoded area on cat head is
white #41 Continental Stitches
╱ Black #00 Backstitch
╱ Christmas green #28 Backstitch
╱ Attach tongue
╱ Attach nose to muzzle
● Attach cat whiskers
╱ Attach muzzle spacer
Color numbers given are for Uniek Needloft
plastic canvas yarn.

Cat Muzzle Spacer
27 holes x 2 holes
Cut 1

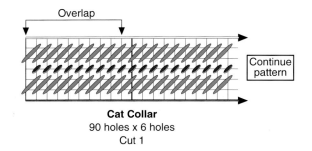

Overlap

Continue
pattern

Cat Collar
90 holes x 6 holes
Cut 1

Cat & Dog Tongue
5 holes x 7 holes
Cut 2

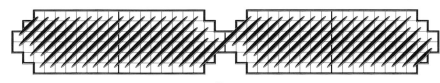

Bow
40 holes x 6 holes
Cut 2
Stitch 1 as graphed for cat
Stitch 1 with Christmas green for dog

Friendship Bookmarks

Give a small token of your affection to a dear friend with one of these heartwarming and quick-to-stitch bookmarks.

See photo on page 49.

The Heart of a Friend Is True

Skill Level
Beginner

Materials
- ¼ sheet ecru 14-count plastic canvas
- DMC #5 pearl cotton as listed in color key
- Rhode Island Textile RibbonFloss as listed in color key
- #24 tapestry needle
- ⅝"-wide grosgrain ribbon:
  ½ yard blue
  ½ yard red

Instructions

1. Cut plastic canvas according to graph. Back piece will remain unstitched.

2. Cross Stitch letters with pearl cotton and hearts with ribbon floss on front piece following graph.

3. Tie a knot in each end of blue and red ribbon. Place blue ribbon on red ribbon; center vertically between front and back pieces.

4. Using dark cornflower blue and a Running Stitch, stitch back and front together following graph, making sure ribbon lies flat between canvas pieces. ***Note: Running Stitch will be stitched through ribbon.***

Friends Are a Breath of Spring

Skill Level
Beginner

Materials
- ½ sheet ecru 14-count plastic canvas
- DMC 6-strand embroidery floss as listed in color key
- #24 tapestry needle
- ⅝"-wide grosgrain ribbon:
  ½ yard blue
  ½ yard yellow
- Ecru sewing thread

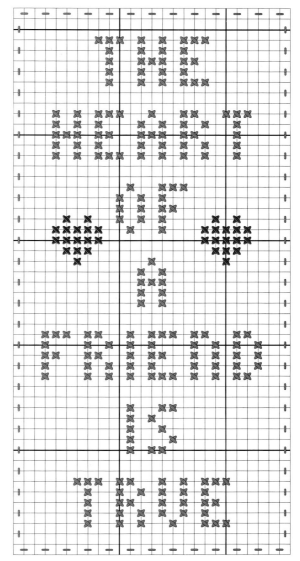

The Heart of a Friend Is True
26 holes x 52 holes
Cut 2, stitch 1

COLOR KEY
THE HEART OF A FRIEND IS TRUE

#5 Pearl Cotton	Yards
■ Dark cornflower blue #798	5
— Dark cornflower blue #798 Running Stitch	
Ribbon Floss	
■ Red #142F-12	1

Color numbers given are for DMC #5 pearl cotton and Rhode Island Textile RibbonFloss.

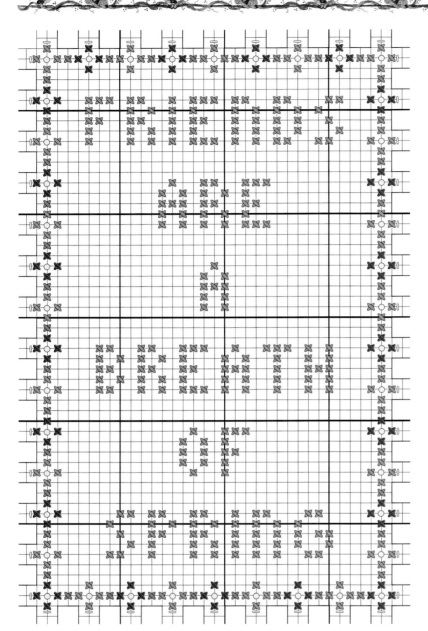

Friends Are a Breath of Spring
38 holes x 58 holes
Cut 2, stitch 1

Stitch, stitch back and front together following graph, making sure ribbon lies flat between canvas pieces. *Note: Running Stitch will be stitched through ribbon.*

Friends Bloom Forever

Skill Level
Beginner

Materials
- ¼ sheet ecru 14-count plastic canvas
- DMC #5 pearl cotton as listed in color key
- #24 tapestry needle
- ¾ yard ⅝"-wide blue grosgrain ribbon
- Ceramic flowerpot button #86081 from Mill Hill Products by Gay Bowles Sales, Inc.
- Green sewing thread to match leaves on button

Instructions
1. Cut plastic canvas according to graph. Back piece will remain unstitched.

2. Cross Stitch letters and border on front piece following graph. With green sewing thread, sew button to front where indicated on graph.

3. Tie a knot in each end of blue ribbon. Crisscross ribbon at center of length, forming a loop. Center ribbon between front and back pieces so that top edge of plastic canvas is at bottom of ribbon loop.

4. Using blue pearl cotton and a Running Stitch, stitch back and front together following graph, making sure ribbon lies flat between canvas pieces. *Note: Running Stitch will be stitched through ribbon.*

Designed by Linda Wyszynski

Instructions
1. Cut plastic canvas according to graph, making sure to leave nubs as indicated for lacy edge. Back piece will remain unstitched.

2. Following graph, Cross Stitch letters, flowers and leaves with 4 strands floss. Work French Knots with 3 strands floss.

3. Tie a knot in each end of blue and yellow ribbon. Place yellow ribbon on blue ribbon; center vertically between front and back pieces.

4. Using 2 strands ecru sewing thread and a Running

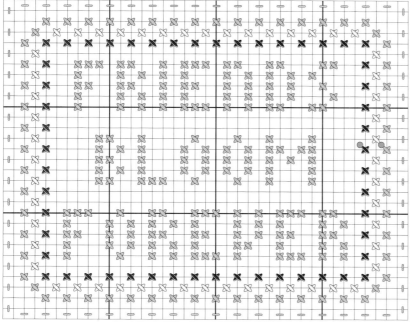

COLOR KEY
FRIENDS BLOOM FOREVER
#5 Pearl Cotton   **Yards**
■ Dark salmon #347   1
□ Light topaz #726   1
▨ Delft #809   6
⁃ Delft #809 Running Stitch
● Attach button
Color numbers given are for DMC
#5 pearl cotton.

Friends Bloom Forever
38 holes x 30 holes
Cut 2, stitch 1

My Pals Photo Frame

School-aged children will love having this colorful frame for displaying their best friends' school pictures!

Skill Level
Beginner

Materials
- ½ sheet red 7-count plastic canvas
- J. & P. Coats Article E.48 100 percent acrylic craft yarn as listed in color key
- 3 ceramic crayon buttons from Mill Hill Products by Gay Bowles Sales, Inc.
- Red sewing thread and needle
- Sawtooth hanger or small magnet
- Hot-glue gun (optional)

Instructions

1. Cut plastic canvas according to graphs.

2. Stitch pieces following graphs. Do not Overcast edges on frame. Overcast letter block A with purple, letter block B with orange, letter block C with tangerine and letter block D with yellow.

3. Using photo as a guide, sew buttons to letter blocks A, C and D, then sew letter blocks to frame with red sewing thread.

4. Carefully center and glue photographs behind each opening.

5. Sew sawtooth hanger or glue magnets to back of frame as desired.

Designed by Judi Kauffman

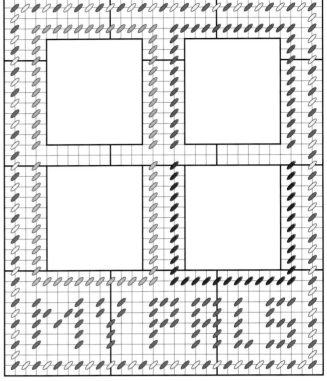

Photo Frame
30 holes x 36 holes
Cut 1

Letter Block A
6 holes x 8 holes
Cut 1

Letter Block B
6 holes x 8 holes
Cut 1

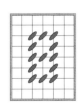

Letter Block C
6 holes x 8 holes
Cut 1

Letter Block D
6 holes x 8 holes
Cut 1

COLOR KEY	
Craft Yarn	**Yards**
☐ Yellow #230	2½
▨ Orange #245	1½
■ Tangerine #253	1½
▨ Purple #596	1½
▨ Emerald green #676	1½
■ Olympic blue #849	3
Uncoded areas are bright red #901 Continental Stitches	7
Color numbers given are for J. & P. Coats 100 percent acrylic craft yarn Article E.48.	

Pocketful of Posies

Instructions begin on page 54

Christmas Rose Pin

Christmas Rose Pin

Delicate embroidered roses and a lacy edge make this pin an elegant gift sure to be remembered and worn for many years to come.

Skill Level
Advanced

Materials
- Scraps 14-count plastic canvas
- DMC 6-strand embroidery floss as listed in color key
- 6" ½"-wide pre-gathered off-white scallop-edge lace
- 1¼" pin back
- Low-temperature glue gun

Project Note
Use 6 strands embroidery floss unless otherwise stated.

Instructions
1. Cut plastic canvas according to graphs.

2. Stitch top and base pieces with Alternating Continental Stitches following graphs. Overcast base with medium dark shell pink and top with ecru.

3. When background stitching and Overcasting are completed, stitch embroidery following embroidery chart. Work Backstitches for stems first with 2 strands blue green. Next work roses, beginning with shell pink French Knots. Working out from center French Knot and overlapping stitches to create dimension, Backstitch first with shell pink then with medium shell pink. When roses are completed, work blue green leaves, then medium dark shell pink French Knots for buds.

4. Glue lace around edge on wrong side of base. Center and glue wrong side of top to right side of base. Center and glue pin back to wrong side of base.

Designed by Celia Lange Designs

Rose Pin Base
23 holes x 17 holes
Cut 1

COLOR KEY	
6-Strand Embroidery Floss	**Yards**
☐ Ecru	3
▨ Medium dark shell pink #221	3
▨ Medium shell pink #223	2
☐ Shell pink #225	3
⟋ Medium shell pink #223 Backstitch	
⟋ Shell pink #225 Backstitch	
⟋ Blue green #502 2-strand Backstitch	1
⟋ Blue green #502 6-strand Backstitch	
● Medium dark shell pink #221 French Knot	
○ Shell pink #225 French Knot	
⟋ Blue green #502 Lazy Daisy	
Color numbers given are for DMC 6-strand embroidery floss.	

Continue pattern

Top Embroidery Chart

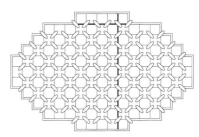

Rose Pin Top
17 holes x 11 holes
Cut 1

Pocketful of Posies

Stitch this pretty heart-shaped flower pocket trimmed with lace in just a couple of hours for a friend who appreciates feminine decor. See photo on page 52.

Skill Level
Beginner

Materials
- 6" 7-count plastic canvas heart by Uniek
- ¼ sheet Uniek Quick-Count 7-count plastic canvas
- Spinrite plastic canvas yarn as listed in color key
- 18" DMC 6-strand ecru embroidery floss
- 24" 1"-wide pre-gathered cream lace
- Pink and ivory silk roses and leaves
- Small amount Spanish moss

Instructions
1. Cut plastic canvas according to graph.

2. Stitch pieces following graphs, using two strands yarn per hole for thistle Straight Stitches and one strand for natural Continental Stitches.

3. With thistle, Overcast the top edge of the front. Place wrong side of front on right side of heart back, aligning edges at bottom of heart. With natural, Whipstitch front to back, beginning at bottom point and Overcasting upper edges of back while Whipstitching.

4. Using 2 strands floss and beginning at bottom point, tack lace around heart, following placement line on front graph and covering natural Overcast Stitches around upper heart edges.

5. Arrange flowers and Spanish moss in pocket as desired. Hang as desired.

Designed by Dianne Davis

COLOR KEY
Plastic Canvas Yarn	Yards
☐ Natural #0002	6
╱ Thistle #0052 Straight Stitch	30
╱ Attach lace	

Color numbers given are for Spinrite plastic canvas yarn.

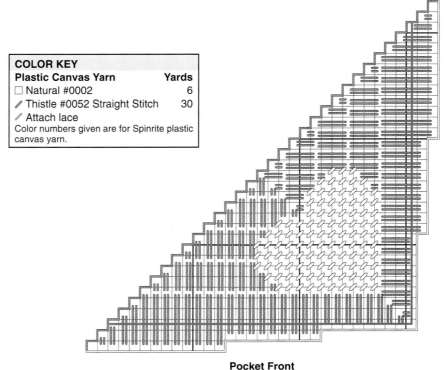

Pocket Front
33 holes x 33 holes
Cut 1

Heart Back
Stitch 1

Christmas Quilt
Table Ensemble

Instructions begin on page 58

Holiday Entertaining

Christmas Quilt Table Ensemble

This handy kitchen set, including place mat, napkin ring and coaster, is sure to add a festive touch to any meal during the holiday season! See photo on page 56.

Skill Level
Beginner

Materials
- 1¼ (12" x 18") sheets 7-count Darice Super Soft plastic canvas
- Uniek Needloft plastic canvas yarn as listed in color key
- #16 tapestry needle

Instructions

1. Cut plastic canvas according to graphs.

2. Stitch pieces following graphs, overlapping four holes on short edges of napkin ring before stitching.

3. Following place mat graph with the end on the left and the center on the right, stitch plastic canvas to center row of holes. Turn graph so the center is on the left and the end is on the right; continue stitching from center row of holes until mat is completed.

4. Overcast all edges with eggshell.

Designed by Angie Arickx

Christmas Quilt Coaster
23 holes x 23 holes
Cut 1

COLOR KEY	
Plastic Canvas Yarn	**Yards**
■ Violet #04	14
■ Forest #29	15
□ Eggshell #39	102
▨ Crimson #42	48
Color numbers given are for Uniek Needloft plastic canvas yarn.	

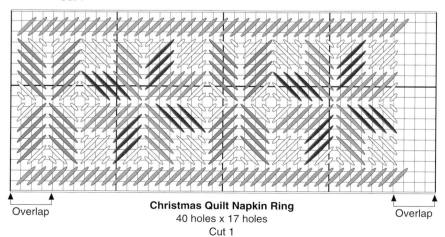

Overlap   Overlap
Christmas Quilt Napkin Ring
40 holes x 17 holes
Cut 1

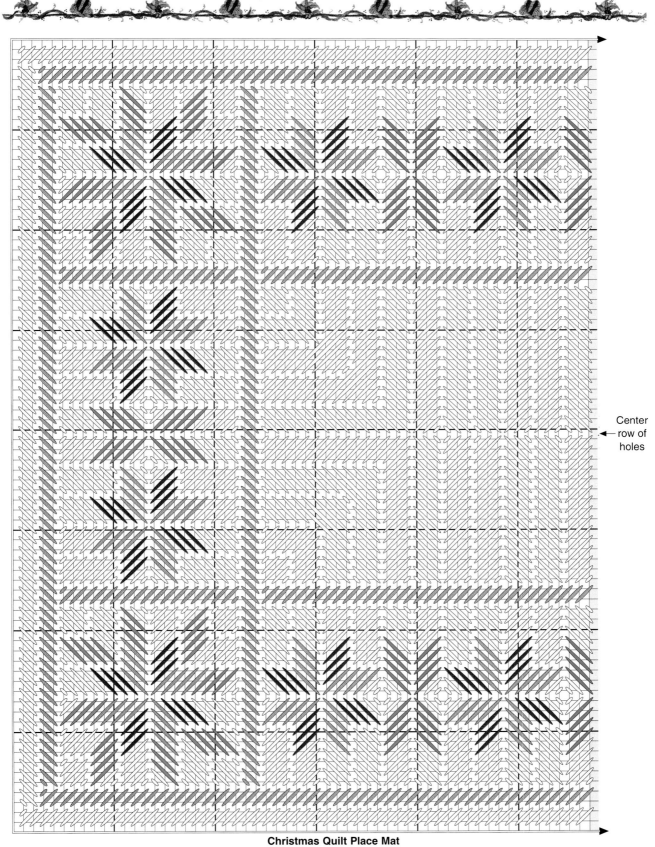

Center
row of
holes

Christmas Quilt Place Mat
115 holes x 79 holes
Cut 1
Stitch first half as shown
Turn graph and stitch second half

Silhouette Cardinal Candlesticks

Give Christmas dinner a touch of elegance with this pair of stately silhouette cardinal candlesticks.

Skill Level
Beginner

Materials
- 1 sheet 7-count Darice Ultra Stiff plastic canvas
- Uniek Needloft plastic canvas yarn as listed in color key
- #18 tapestry needle
- 2 (7mm) opaque black round cabochons by The Beadery
- 9" x 12" piece black felt
- 2 (12") lengths ½"-diameter wooden dowels
- 2 large wooden colonial candle cups
- 2 (4"-diameter x ¾"-thick) wooden wheels
- 2 small sprays metallic Christmas flowers
- Black semigloss enamel paint
- Small paintbrush
- Wood glue
- Tacky craft glue

Instructions
1. Cut plastic canvas according to graph. Using cardinals as templates, cut felt slightly smaller than birds. Cut circles from felt to fit bottom of wheels.

2. Stitch pieces following graph, reversing one cardinal before stitching. Overcast with black. With tacky glue, glue felt to back of birds.

3. With wood glue, glue dowels into center of wheels. Glue candle cups to tops of dowels. Allow to dry.

4. With small brush, paint candlesticks with three to four coats of black paint. Allow to dry between coats. Allow to dry completely after last coat.

5. With tacky glue, glue felt circles to bottoms of wheels. Using photo as a guide through step 6, glue cardinals to dowels.

6. After removing stems, glue flowers and leaves around base of candlestick. Glue flower and leaves and black cabochon to front of cardinals where indicated on graph.

Designed by Vicki Blizzard

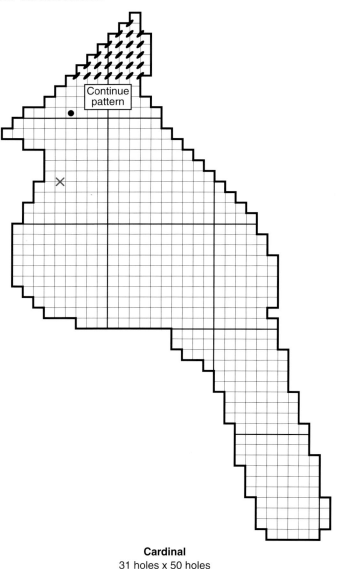

Cardinal
31 holes x 50 holes
Cut 2, reverse 1

Continue pattern

Poinsettia Bread Basket

Place fresh-from-the oven crescent rolls, cinnamon buns or muffins in this pretty bread basket adorned with holly and poinsettias!

Skill Level
Intermediate

Materials
- 12" x 18" sheet 7-count Darice Super Soft plastic canvas
- Uniek Needloft plastic canvas yarn as listed in color key
- #16 tapestry needle
- Wicker basket with 24"–26"-long handle
- Hot-glue gun

Instructions

1. Cut plastic canvas according to graphs.

2. Stitch and Overcast pieces following graphs. While stitching holly vines, overlap three holes of the two pieces where indicated to form one long vine. Work Backstitches and French Knots when background stitching and Overcasting are completed.

3. Following photo and Fig. 1, glue poinsettia pieces together, then glue poinsettias to rim of basket at handles. Wind holly vine around handle, securing ends with glue.

Designed by Angie Arickx

COLOR KEY	
Plastic Canvas Yarn	**Yards**
☐ Holly #27	40
☐ Crimson #42	25
✏ Violet #04 Backstitch	5
✏ Forest #29 Backstitch	13
○ Straw #19 French Knot	2
● Crimson #42 French Knot	
Color numbers given are for Uniek Needloft plastic canvas yarn.	

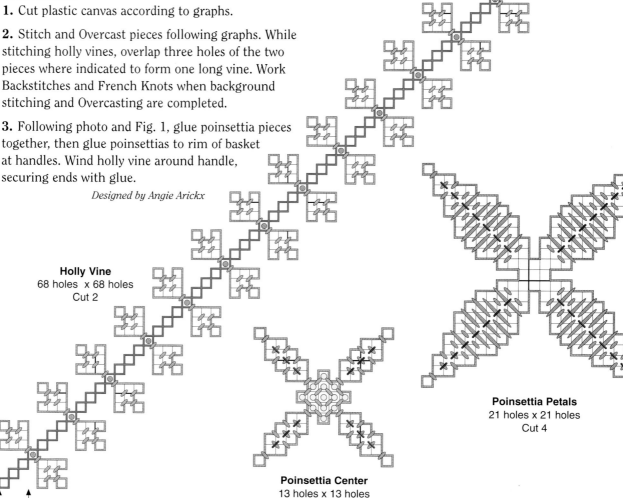

Holly Vine
68 holes x 68 holes
Cut 2

Poinsettia Petals
21 holes x 21 holes
Cut 4

Poinsettia Center
13 holes x 13 holes
Cut 2

Overlap

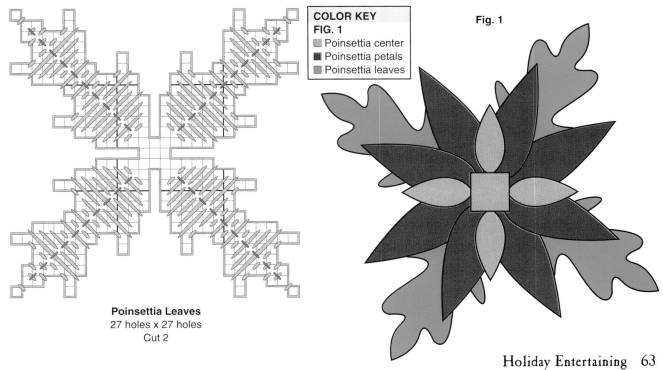

**COLOR KEY
FIG. 1**
▨ Poinsettia center
◼ Poinsettia petals
▨ Poinsettia leaves

Fig. 1

Poinsettia Leaves
27 holes x 27 holes
Cut 2

Country Buffet Helpers

These colorful coasters and silverware rings are perfect for a large buffet dinner! Serve up mugs of hot apple cider on the coasters and wrap silverware in a linen napkin with a silverware ring holding it all together!

Skill Level
Beginner

Materials
- 1 sheet 7-count plastic canvas
- Small amount 10-count plastic canvas
- Darice Nylon Plus plastic canvas yarn as listed in color key
- DMC #3 pearl cotton as listed in color key
- Small amount 6-strand embroidery floss as listed in color key
- Sheet white Fun Foam craft foam by Westrim Crafts
- 4 (1¼") strips white hook-and-loop tape
- Sewing needle and white thread
- Low-temperature glue gun

Instructions

1. Cut coasters and silverware napkin rings from 7-count plastic canvas and heart, goose, pineapple and house from 10-count plastic canvas according to graphs (pages 66 and 67). Cut four pieces of craft foam slightly smaller than coasters.

2. Stitch 7-count pieces with yarn and 10-count pieces with pearl cotton following graphs. Work embroidery when background stitching is completed, using 2 strands black floss for French Knot on goose.

3. Overcast coasters and silverware napkin rings with baby green. Glue craft foam to backs of coasters. Overcast 10-count pieces following graphs, then glue to center fronts of silverware napkin rings.

4. Sew hook side of tape to front on left edge of holder; sew loop side of tape to backside on right edge of holder.

5. Wrap silverware for buffet in napkin and wrap ring around napkin, securing with hook-and-loop tape.

Designed by Celia Lange Designs

COLOR KEY	
Plastic Canvas Yarn	**Yards**
☐ White #01	12
■ Burgundy #13	10
▨ Gold #27	5
▨ Forest green #32	12
☐ Christmas green #58	12
Uncoded areas are baby green #28	
Continental Stitches	40
⁄ Baby green #28 Overcasting	
⁄ Forest green #32 Backstitch	
#3 Pearl Cotton	
☐ White	3
▨ Medium shell pink #223	2
▨ Golden mustard #832	3
▨ Ultra dark pistachio green #890	4
■ Very dark garnet #902	3
▨ Willow green #904	5
⁄ Ultra dark pistachio green #890 Backstitch	
⁄ Willow green #904 Backstitch	
6-Strand Embroidery Floss	
● Black #310 French Knot	
Color numbers given are for Darice Nylon Plus plastic canvas yarn and DMC #3 pearl cotton and 6-strand embroidery floss.	

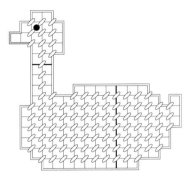

Country Buffet Goose
16 holes x 15 holes
Cut 1 from 10-count
Stitch with pearl cotton and floss

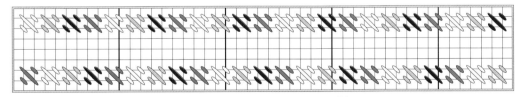

Country Buffet Silverware Napkin Ring
47 holes x 8 holes
Cut 4 from 7-count
Stitch with yarn

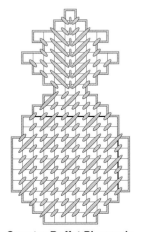

Country Buffet Pineapple
11 holes x 20 holes
Cut 1 from 10-count
Stitch with pearl cotton

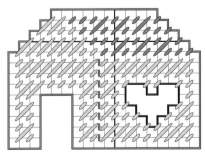

Country Buffet House
18 holes x 13 holes
Cut 1 from 10-count
Stitch with pearl cotton

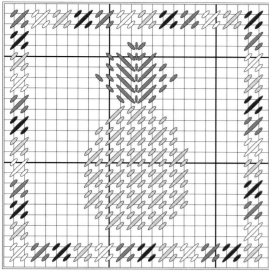

Country Buffet Pineapple Coaster
25 holes x 25 holes
Cut 1 from 7-count
Stitch with yarn

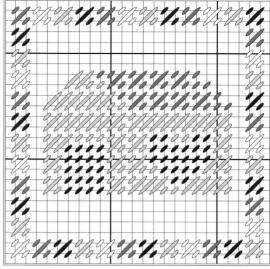

Country Buffet House Coaster
25 holes x 25 holes
Cut 1 from 7-count
Stitch with yarn

Country Buffet Heart
15 holes x 13 holes
Cut 1 from 10-count
Stitch with pearl cotton

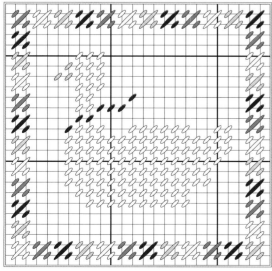

Country Buffet Goose Coaster
25 holes x 25 holes
Cut 1 from 7-count
Stitch with yarn

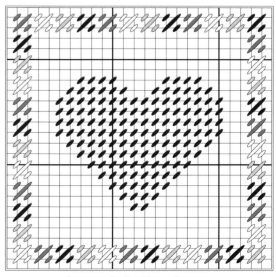

Country Buffet Heart Coaster
25 holes x 25 holes
Cut 1 from 7-count
Stitch with yarn

Welcome Wreath

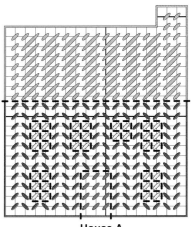

Quaint cottages filled with warmth and cheer decorate this wintry wreath. Hang it on your front door to invite Christmas guests inside!

Skill Level
Beginner

Materials
- 2 sheets 7-count Darice Ultra Stiff plastic canvas
- Darice Nylon Plus plastic canvas yarn as listed in color key
- DMC 6-strand embroidery floss as listed in color key
- 14"-diameter plastic foam wreath form
- Polyester fiberfill
- Raffia
- Artificial evergreen sprigs
- Low-temperature glue gun

Instructions
1. Cut plastic canvas according to graphs.

2. Stitch pieces following graphs. Overcast pieces following graphs. Work embroidery with 6 strands floss when background stitching and Overcasting are completed.

3. Wrap wreath with fiberfill. Using photo as a guide through step 4, wrap raffia around fiberfill and tie in bows.

4. Place evergreen behind houses on wreath; glue in place.

Designed by Celia Lange Designs

COLOR KEY	
Plastic Canvas Yarn	**Yards**
☐ Sail blue #04	2
■ Cinnamon #20	7
☐ Eggshell #24	7
▨ Holly green #31	9
■ Forest green #32	5
▨ Maple #35	3
▨ Cerulean #38	1
☐ Straw #41	3
▨ Bark #44	3
▨ Crimson #53	4
Uncoded areas are denim #06 Continental Stitches	5
⁄ Denim #06 Overcasting	
6-Strand Embroidery Floss	
⁄ Black #310 Backstitch	3
⁄ Ultra dark coffee brown #938 Backstitch	5
Color numbers given are for Darice Nylon Plus plastic canvas yarn and DMC 6-strand embroidery floss.	

House A
18 holes x 21 holes
Cut 1

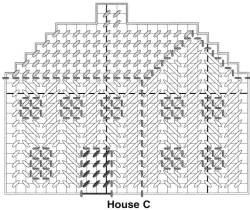

House C
24 holes x 19 holes
Cut 1

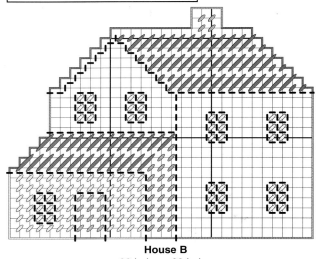

House B
30 holes x 23 holes
Cut 1

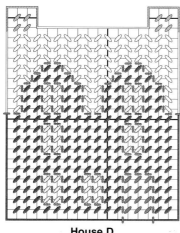

House D
17 holes x 21 holes
Cut 1

House E
17 holes x 19 holes
Cut 2

Gingerbread Cookie Tin

Here's a great gift idea for the postman! Bake a batch of delicious gingerbread cookies, then give it to him in this adorable decorated cookie tin! He'll love it!

Skill Level
Beginner

Materials
- ⅔ sheet 7-count plastic canvas
- Spinrite Bernat Berella "4" worsted weight yarn as listed in color key
- Spinrite plastic canvas yarn as listed in color key
- #16 tapestry needle
- 8"-diameter metal cookie tin
- 18" ⅛"-wide red satin ribbon
- ½" tan 2-hole button
- Sewing needle and tan thread
- Hot-glue gun

Instructions

1. Cut plastic canvas according to graph.

2. Stitch piece following graph. Work embroidery with 2 plies yarn over completed background stitching. Overcast with dark lagoon.

3. Sew button to heart where indicated on graph. Cut ribbon in half. Thread one length of ribbon from front to back on each gingerbread person through holes indicated on graph. Tie each ribbon in a bow at neckline, trimming ends as desired.

4. Glue finished piece to top of cookie tin lid.

Designed by Joan Green

COLOR KEY

Worsted Weight Yarn	Yards
▨ Medium gold #8811	7
▨ Medium lagoon #8821	12
▨ Arbutus #8922	½
■ Geranium #8929	5
Uncoded areas are dark lagoon #8822 Continental Stitches	18
⁄ Dark lagoon #8822 Overcasting	
⁄ Winter white #8941 2-ply Backstitch	2
✓ Black #8994 2-ply Backstitch	½
○ Winter white #8941 2-ply French Knot	
● Black #8994 2-ply French Knot	
Plastic Canvas Yarn	
▨ Wine #0011	1
◎ Attach button	
● Attach ribbon	

Color numbers given are for Spinrite Bernat Berella "4" worsted weight yarn and plastic canvas yarn.

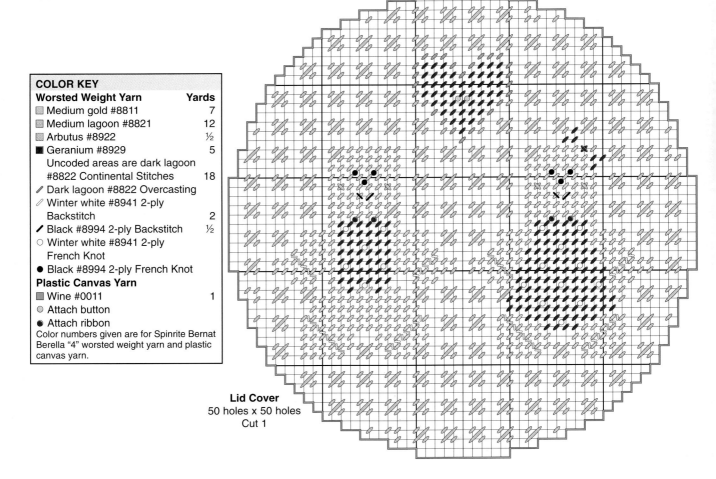

Lid Cover
50 holes x 50 holes
Cut 1

Elfin Santas

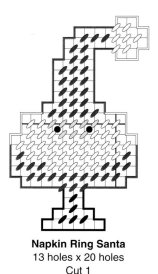

Stitch up this place mat and napkin ring set featuring whimsical Santas sure to bring a smile to your face!

Skill Level
Beginner

Materials
- 1¼ sheets 7-count plastic canvas
- Uniek Needloft plastic canvas yarn as listed in color key
- DMC #3 pearl cotton as listed in color key
- Hot-glue gun

Instructions

1. Cut plastic canvas according to graphs (below and page 74). Place mat will use one 90-hole x 70-hole sheet.

2. Stitch pieces following graphs. Stitch seven uncoded areas on place mat following the one Santa area given. Work French Knots over completed background stitching.

3. Overcast place mat with crimson, long sides of napkin ring with Christmas green and Santa with adjacent colors.

4. Whipstitch short sides of napkin ring together with holly. Using photo as a guide, glue Santa to napkin ring.

Designed by Michele Wilcox

Napkin Ring Santa
13 holes x 20 holes
Cut 1

Continue pattern

Napkin Ring
8 holes x 40 holes
Cut 1

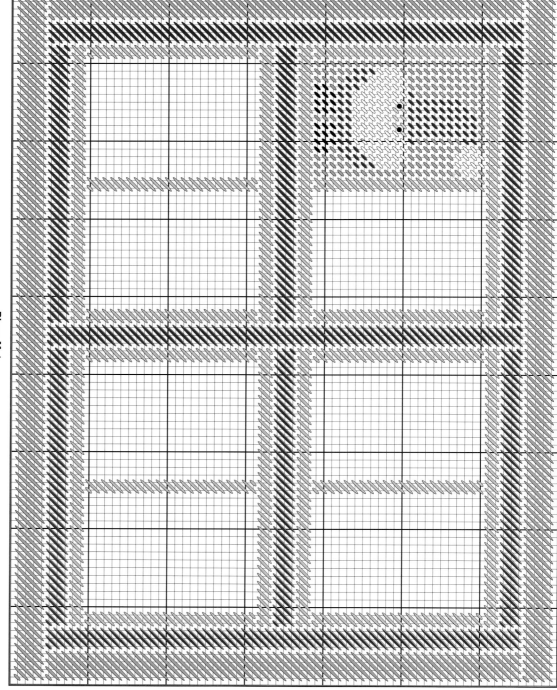

Place Mat
90 holes x 70 holes
Cut 1
Stitch uncoded areas with Santa
motif given

COLOR KEY	
Plastic Canvas Yarn	**Yards**
■ Black #00	6
▨ Tangerine #11	16
▨ Christmas green #28	45
☐ White #41	12
■ Crimson #42	27
▨ Flesh tone #56	4
#3 Pearl Cotton	
● Black #310 French Knot	2
Color numbers given are for Uniek Needloft	
plastic canvas yarn and DMC #3 pearl cotton.	

Christmas Tree Coasters

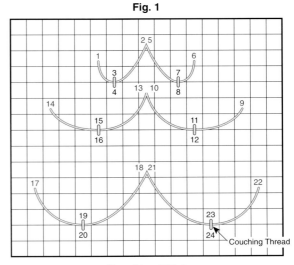

Festive, fun and a cinch to stitch, this set of coasters with holder will delight all your holiday guests!

Skill Level
Beginner

Materials
- 1 sheet 7-count plastic canvas
- Darice Nylon Plus plastic canvas yarn as listed in color key
- Kreinik Medium (#16) Braid as listed in color key
- 4 (⅜") 2-hole white pearl buttons
- 9" x 12" piece kelly green felt
- 5" x 5" piece white felt
- Hot-glue gun or craft glue

Instructions

1. Cut plastic canvas according to graphs (below and page 76). Box bottom will remain unstitched.

2. Using coasters as templates, cut four pieces of green felt slightly smaller than coasters. Using coaster box bottom as a template, cut white felt slightly larger than bottom.

3. Stitch the pieces following the graphs, adding red French Knots over completed background stitching. Following Fig. 1 and coaster graph, work pearl braid Couching Stitches.

4. Overcast the coasters with holly green. Using white throughout, Overcast the top edges of the box sides with white. Whipstitch the ends of the box short side to the ends of the box long side. Whipstitch the box bottom to the box sides. *Note: There will be holes on the bottom piece that do not line up with the sides, creating small openings.*

5. Using pearl braid, sew one button to each coaster where indicated on graph.

6. Glue one piece green felt to back of each coaster. Place felt inside box, covering bottom and holes.

Designed by Linda Wyszynski

Fig. 1

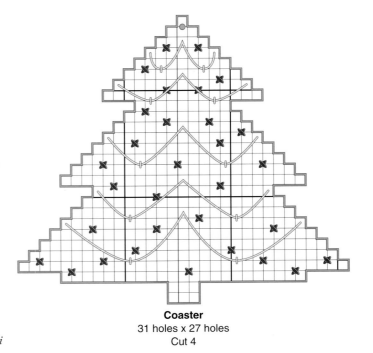

Couching Stitch
Bring needle up at 1, down at 2,
up at 3, down at 4, etc.

Coaster
31 holes x 27 holes
Cut 4

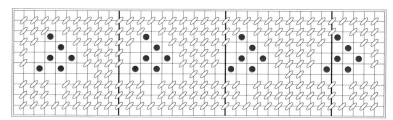

Box Short Side
35 holes x 10 holes
Cut 1

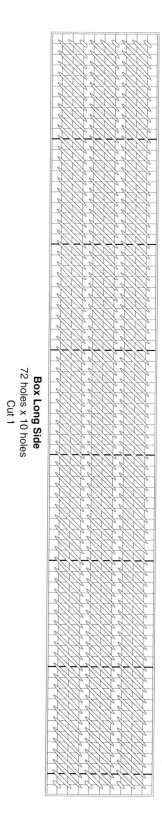

Box Long Side
72 holes x 10 holes
Cut 1

COLOR KEY	
Plastic Canvas Yarn	**Yards**
☐ White #01	20
Uncoded areas are holly green	
#31 Continental Stitches	22
╱ Holly green #31 Overcasting	
Medium (#16) Braid	
■ Red #003	11
● Red #003 French Knot	
∪ Pearl #032 Couching Stitch	5
● Attach button	
Color numbers given are for Darice Nylon Plus plastic canvas yarn and Kreinik Medium (#16) Braid.	

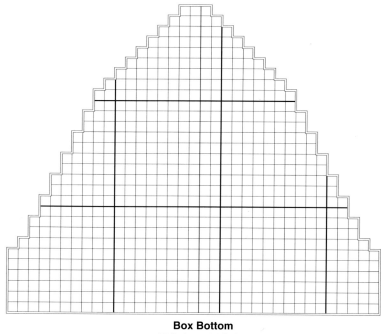

Box Bottom
35 holes x 29 holes
Cut 1
Do not stitch

Winter Luminaries
Instructions on page 80

Dressing Up The Mantel

Winter Luminaries

A decorated Christmas tree and charming cottage are quaint decorations by day and enchanting luminaries by night. See photo on pages 78 and 79.

Skill Level
Intermediate

Materials
- 3 sheets 7-count Darice Ultra Stiff plastic canvas
- Scraps 7-count black plastic canvas
- Darice Nylon Plus plastic canvas yarn as listed in color key
- 1" frosted sisal wreath
- Darice Jewelry Designer Fancy Jewel 20mm clear star
- Assorted miniatures
- Small amount miniature artificial pine stem
- 2 votive candles with plain glass holders
- Yellow sheet Fun Foam craft foam by Westrim Crafts
- Low-temperature glue gun

Project Note
Miniatures on sample tree luminary are sled, hobby horse and pegboard.

Cutting & Stitching
1. Cut windows from black plastic canvas and remaining pieces from clear stiff plastic canvas according to graphs (also see page 82). Cut out holes on base tops only. Cut out blue lines on leaded windows, leaving black lines only. Windows will remain unstitched.

2. Using cottage and tree as templates, cut yellow craft foam slightly smaller than cottage and tree for backing.

3. Stitch pieces following graphs, stitching one large brace with Christmas green and two large braces with beige. Overcast inside edges of tree with Christmas green. Overcast inside edges of door window with crimson and inside edges of cottage windows with maple. Overcast outside edges of cottage with beige. Overcast braces with adjacent colors.

COLOR KEY

Plastic Canvas Yarn	Yards
☐ White #01	68
☐ Sail blue #04	2
■ Cinnamon #20	3
☐ Maple #35	5
☐ Straw #41	2
☐ Moss #48	2
☐ Crimson #53	3
☐ Christmas green #58	15
Uncoded areas on tree are Christmas green #58 Continental Stitches	
Uncoded areas on cottage are beige #43 Continental Stitches	12
✎ Beige #43 Overcasting	
✎ Attach cottage and tree	

Color numbers given are for Darice Nylon Plus plastic canvas yarn.

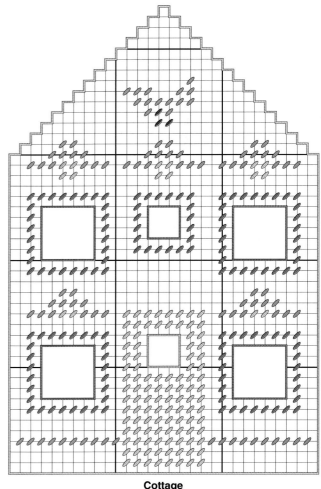

Cottage
29 holes x 44 holes
Cut 1 from clear

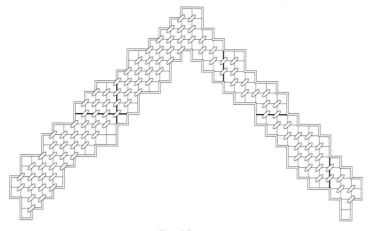

Roof Snow
33 holes x 20 holes
Cut 1 from clear

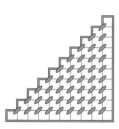

Large Brace
10 holes x 10 holes
Cut 3 from clear
Stitch 1 as graphed for tree
Stitch 2 with beige for cottage

Tree Small Brace
7 holes x 7 holes
Cut 2 from clear

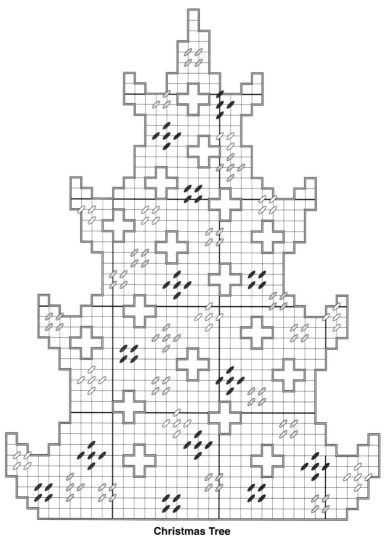

Christmas Tree
35 holes x 48 holes
Cut 1 from clear

4. Using white through step 5, Overcast door snowcap and roof snow. Whipstitch one long edge of step top to one long edge of step front; Overcast remaining step edges.

5. Overcast inside edges of base tops. Place wrong side of one base top on right side of one base bottom; Whipstitch together. Repeat with remaining base pieces.

Assembly

1. Using photo as a guide through step 5, glue leaded windows behind four large window openings on backside of cottage. Glue yellow craft foam to back of cottage.

2. Glue roof snow to top front of cottage. Glue cottage braces to back side edges of cottage, making sure side and bottom edges are even. Center and glue cottage and braces to base top where indicated on graph.

3. Center and glue step to base and cottage in front of door. Glue wreath to front door so window shows through center of wreath. Glue door snowcap above wreath to top of door. Glue pine stem together, forming two bushes;

glue bushes to base and cottage at cottage corners.

4. Glue yellow craft foam to back of tree. Glue star to treetop. Making sure bottom edges are even, glue large tree brace to center back of tree, then glue small braces approximately 1¼" from large brace on each side.

5. Center and glue tree to base top where indicated on graph. Glue miniatures as desired in front of tree.

6. Place candles in holders; place holders in base top openings.

Designed by Celia Lange Designs

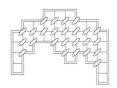

Door Snowcap
9 holes x 7 holes
Cut 1 from clear

Step Top & Front
11 holes x 2 holes
Cut 2 from clear

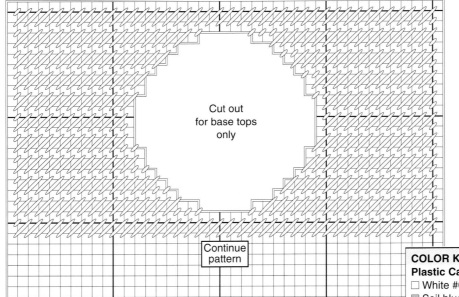

Cut out
for base tops
only

Continue
pattern

Base Top & Bottom
41 holes x 41 holes
Cut 2 base tops from clear
Cut 2 base bottoms from clear

Leaded Window
11 holes x 11 holes
Cut 4 from black
Cut out blue lines,
leaving black lines only
Do not stitch

COLOR KEY	
Plastic Canvas Yarn	**Yards**
☐ White #01	68
▨ Sail blue #04	2
■ Cinnamon #20	3
▨ Maple #35	5
☐ Straw #41	2
▨ Moss #48	2
▨ Crimson #53	3
▨ Christmas green #58	15
Uncoded areas on tree are Christmas green #58 Continental Stitches	
Uncoded areas on cottage are beige #43 Continental Stitches	12
⁄ Beige #43 Overcasting	
⁄ Attach cottage and tree	
Color numbers given are for Darice Nylon Plus plastic canvas yarn.	

Reindeer Match Holder

Chase away those winter chills by lighting a cozy fire in the fireplace. This reindeer project serves double duty as a fireplace mantel decoration and a handy long match holder!

Skill Level

Intermediate

Materials

- 2 sheets 7-count Darice Ultra Stiff plastic canvas
- Darice Nylon Plus plastic canvas yarn as listed in color key
- #16 tapestry needle
- 2 (18mm) brown oval movable eyes
- 7 (10mm) jingle bells
- 1½"–3½"-long twigs
- 2 miniature pinecones
- Long fireplace matches
- Low-temperature glue gun

Instructions

1. Cut plastic canvas according to graphs (also see pages 85 and 86), cutting out hole on base top only.

2. Stitch pieces following graphs. Using white throughout, Overcast inside edges of base top. Place wrong side of base top on right side of base bottom, matching edges; Whipstitch together.

3. With maple, Whipstitch angled edges of support pieces together; Overcast remaining straight edges. Overcast remaining pieces following graphs. Work Backstitches with 2 plies yarn when Overcasting is completed.

4. Following Fig. 1 and using photo as a guide through step 7, glue reindeer together. Making sure bottom edges are even, glue long straight edges of support to center backside of reindeer. Glue tree behind reindeer,

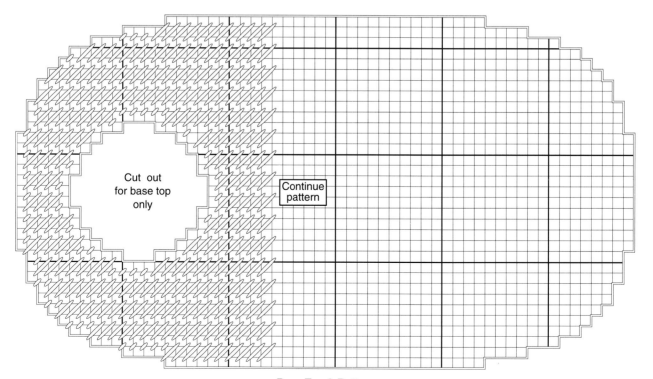

Base Top & Bottom
58 holes x 33 holes
Cut 2

Cut out for base top only

Continue pattern

making sure bottom edges are even.

5. With yarn, sew five jingle bells to collar where indicated on graph, then sew collar ends to backside of reindeer's hooves, making sure jingle bells are facing out.

6. Glue reindeer, tree and support to base top so the collar is above the hole on the base. Glue twigs in two stacks; glue pinecones near one stack.

7. With cinnamon yarn, tie a small bow to antlers, attaching two jingle bells to ends of bow. Glue bow to secure. Tie a small forest green bow and glue between chin and shoulder. Glue eyes to head.

8. Slip matches through collar, placing ends in hole on base top.

Designed by Celia Lange Designs

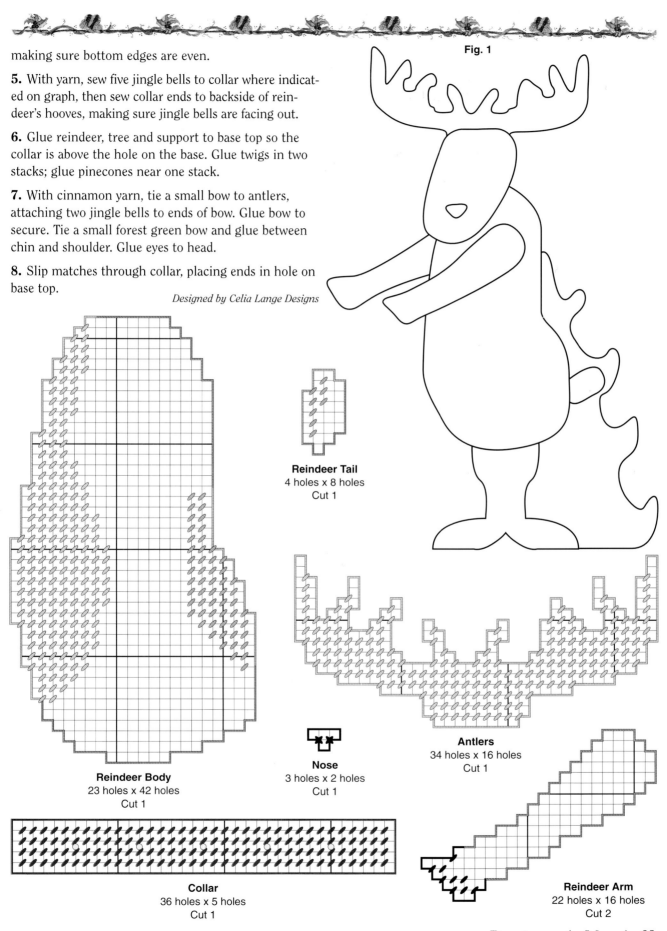

Fig. 1

Reindeer Tail
4 holes x 8 holes
Cut 1

Reindeer Body
23 holes x 42 holes
Cut 1

Nose
3 holes x 2 holes
Cut 1

Antlers
34 holes x 16 holes
Cut 1

Reindeer Arm
22 holes x 16 holes
Cut 2

Collar
36 holes x 5 holes
Cut 1

COLOR KEY

Plastic Canvas Yarn	Yards
☐ White #01	38
▨ Sundown #16	6
■ Cinnamon #20	5
▨ Tan #33	10
■ Bark #44	2
Uncoded areas on tree are forest green #32 Continental Stitches	12
Uncoded areas on support and reindeer pieces are maple #35 Continental Stitches	22
╱ Forest green #32 Overcasting	
╱ Maple #35 Overcasting	
╱ Brown #36 Backstitch	⅙
╱ Bark #44 Backstitch	
○ Attach jingle bell	

Color numbers given are for Darice Nylon Plus plastic canvas yarn.

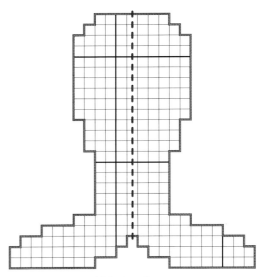

Reindeer Legs
23 holes x 24 holes
Cut 1

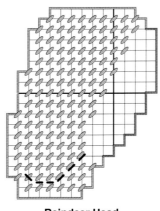

Reindeer Head
14 holes x 18 holes
Cut 1

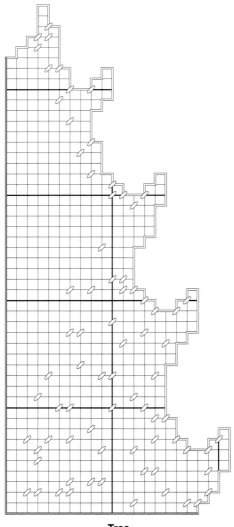

Tree
21 holes x 48 holes
Cut 1

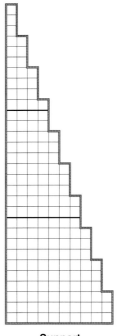

Support
10 holes x 30 holes
Cut 2

Elegant Mantel Runner

Give your fireplace mantel a lustrous, elegant look by covering it with this gorgeous runner. Golden tassels and metallic thread will sparkle in the light!

Skill Level
Beginner

Materials
- 2 sheets 7-count plastic canvas
- Worsted weight yarn as listed in color key
- Plastic Canvas 7 Metallic Needlepoint Yarn by Rainbow Gallery as listed in color key
- #16 tapestry needle
- 3"-long gold metallic tassel
- 2 (2¼"-long) gold metallic tassels
- Hot-glue gun

Instructions

1. Cut plastic canvas according to graphs (see pages 88 and 89).

2. Following graphs, stitch pieces with cream yarn first, then work gold centers in diagonal rows to conserve yarn.

3. Using cream yarn through step 4, Whipstitch one side edge of each small triangle to side edges of large triangle. Whipstitch one side edge of each small rectangle to side edges of large rectangle.

4. Whipstitch bottom edge of rectangular strip to top edge of triangular strip. Overcast all remaining edges.

5. Glue hanger of large tassel to backside of large triangle and hangers of small tassels to backsides of small triangles at points, so that tassels hang freely from points.

Designed by Joan Green

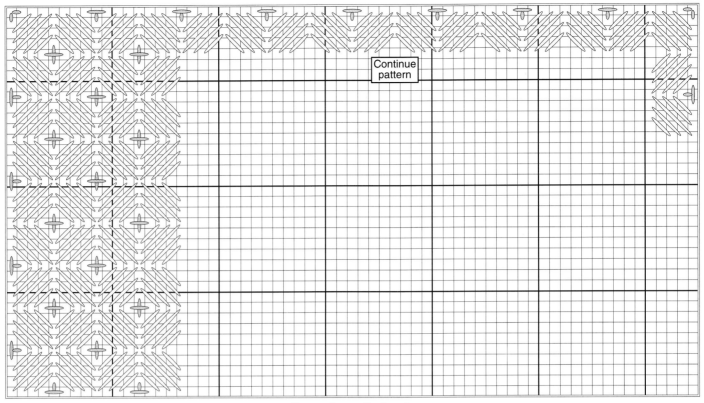

Runner Large Rectangle
65 holes x 37 holes
Cut 1

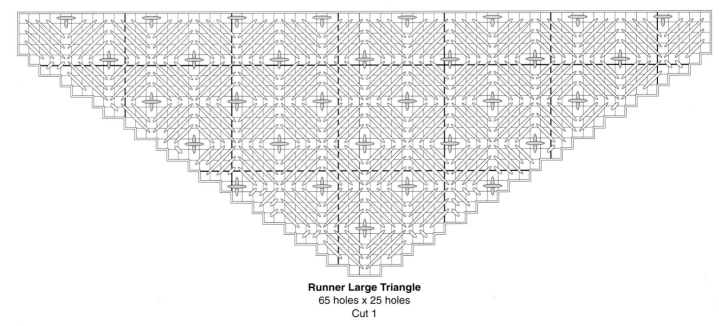

Runner Large Triangle
65 holes x 25 holes
Cut 1

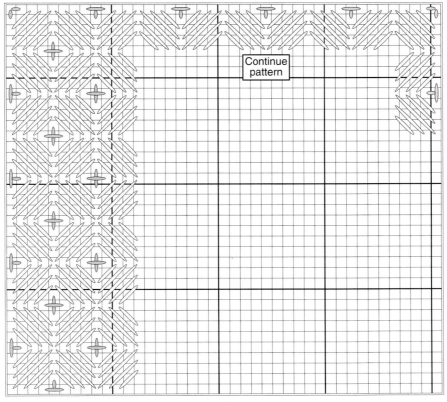

Runner Small Rectangle
41 holes x 37 holes
Cut 2

COLOR KEY	
Worsted Weight Yarn	**Yards**
☐ Cream	75
⅛". Metallic Needlepoint Yarn	
☐ Gold #PC 7	16
Color number given is for Rainbow Gallery Plastic Canvas 7 Metallic Needlepoint Yarn.	

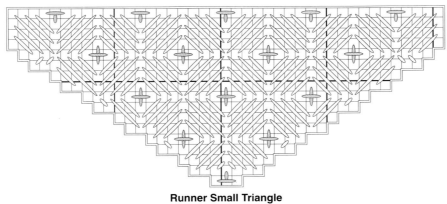

Runner Small Triangle
41 holes x 17 holes
Cut 2

Santa Photo Frame

Display and share one of your fondest Christmas memories in this attractive photo frame decorated with a moon-shaped Santa.

Skill Level
Beginner

Materials
- ⅔ sheet 7-count plastic canvas
- Uniek Needloft plastic canvas yarn as listed in color key
- #3 pearl cotton as listed in color key
- Picture frame (sample used frame for 3½" x 5" photo)
- Hot-glue gun

Instructions

1. Cut plastic canvas according to graphs.

2. Stitch pieces following graphs, adding black French Knot when Continental Stitching is completed. Overcast with adjacent colors.

3. Using photo as a guide, glue mustache under cheek. Glue Santa to frame.

Designed by Michele Wilcox

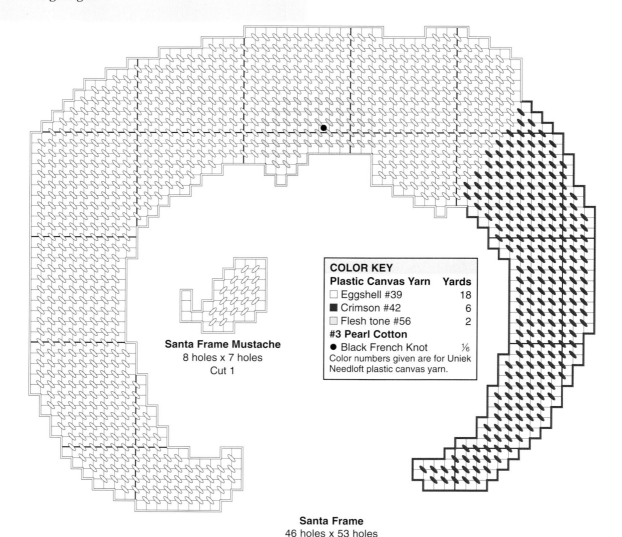

Santa Frame Mustache
8 holes x 7 holes
Cut 1

COLOR KEY	
Plastic Canvas Yarn	**Yards**
☐ Eggshell #39	18
■ Crimson #42	6
☐ Flesh tone #56	2
#3 Pearl Cotton	
● Black French Knot	⅙
Color numbers given are for Uniek Needloft plastic canvas yarn.	

Santa Frame
46 holes x 53 holes
Cut 1

Folk Country Stockings

Three delightful stockings—an angel, Santa and a snowman—will please every member of the family, young and old alike. See additional photos on pages 95 and 96.

Materials

Each Stocking
- 2 sheets 7-count Darice Super Soft plastic canvas
- Spinrite Bernat Berella "4" worsted weight yarn as listed in color key
- #16 tapestry needle
- Gold star button #86016 from Mill Hill Products by Gay Bowles Sales, Inc.
- Sewing needle and matching thread
- 12" ⅞"-wide red satin ribbon

Angel Stocking
- Spinrite plastic canvas yarn as listed in color key
- 6 beige buttons in assorted sizes
- 3 red buttons in assorted sizes

Santa Stocking
- 5 beige buttons in assorted sizes
- 4 red buttons in assorted sizes

Snowman Stocking
- Spinrite plastic canvas yarn as listed in color key
- 6 beige buttons in assorted sizes
- 3 red buttons in assorted sizes

Angel Stocking

1. Cut plastic canvas according to graph (page 98). Stocking back will remain unstitched.

2. Stitch stocking front following graph. When background stitching is completed, work dress-button French Knots with 4 plies black yarn; work all other embroidery with 2 plies yarn.

3. Using photo (left) as a guide and sewing needle and matching thread, sew on buttons as follows: red buttons as desired to tree, gold star to treetop, one beige button to heart center, three beige buttons as desired to toe and two beige buttons as desired to heel.

4. Cut a 4" lengths of dark lagoon yarn. Separate yarn into two 2-ply lengths. Thread one 2-ply length from back to front where indicated on left side of hair. Tie in a bow and trim ends as desired. Repeat with remaining 2-ply length on right side of hair.

5. Matching edges, Whipstitch stocking front to stock-ing back following graph. Thread one end of red ribbon through hole indicated on stocking front. Tie ends in a tight knot. Pull ribbon so knot is hidden inside stocking.

Santa Stocking

1. Cut plastic canvas according to graph (page 94). Stocking back will remain unstitched.

2. Stitch stocking front following graph. Use 4 plies yarn to work French Knots for coat buttons, nose and dots on beard. Work all other embroidery with 2 plies yarn.

3. Using photo (page 95) as a guide and sewing needle and matching thread, sew on buttons as follows: one red button to Santa's bag, three red buttons as desired to tree, gold star to treetop, three beige buttons as desired to toe and two beige buttons as desired to heel.

4. Matching edges, Whipstitch stocking front to stock-ing back following graph. Thread one end of red ribbon through hole indicated on stocking front. Tie ends in a tight knot. Pull ribbon so knot is hidden inside stocking.

Snowman Stocking

1. Cut plastic canvas according to graph (page 97). Stocking back will remain unstitched.

2. Stitch stocking front following graph. Work jacket-button French Knots with 4 plies wine yarn. Work all other embroidery with 2 plies yarn.

3. Using photo (page 96) as a guide and sewing needle and matching thread, sew on buttons as follows: red buttons as desired to tree, gold star to treetop, one beige button for knot on scarf, three beige buttons as desired to toe and two beige buttons as desired to heel.

4. Matching edges, Whipstitch stocking front to stock-ing back following graph. Thread one end of red ribbon through hole indicated on stocking front. Tie ends in a tight knot. Pull ribbon so knot is hidden inside stocking.

Designed by Joan Green

COLOR KEY
SANTA STOCKING

Worsted Weight Yarn	Yards
☐ Honey #8795	2
▨ Periwinkle #8804	12
☐ Medium lagoon #8821	3
▥ Dark lagoon #8822	16
▧ Walnut #8916	½
■ Geranium #8929	12
☐ Winter white #8941	8
☐ Light peach #8977	1
▨ Hunter green #8981	18
■ Black #8994	5

Uncoded areas are winter white
#8941 Continental Stitches
✒ Black #8994 2-ply Backstitch
◉ Rose #8921 2-ply French Knot ½
● Geranium #8929 2-ply French Knot
◉ Geranium #8929 4-ply French Knot
○ Winter white #8941 4-ply French Knot
● Black #8994 4-ply French Knot
○ Attach ribbon hanger
Color numbers given are for Spinrite Bernat Berella
"4" worsted weight yarn.

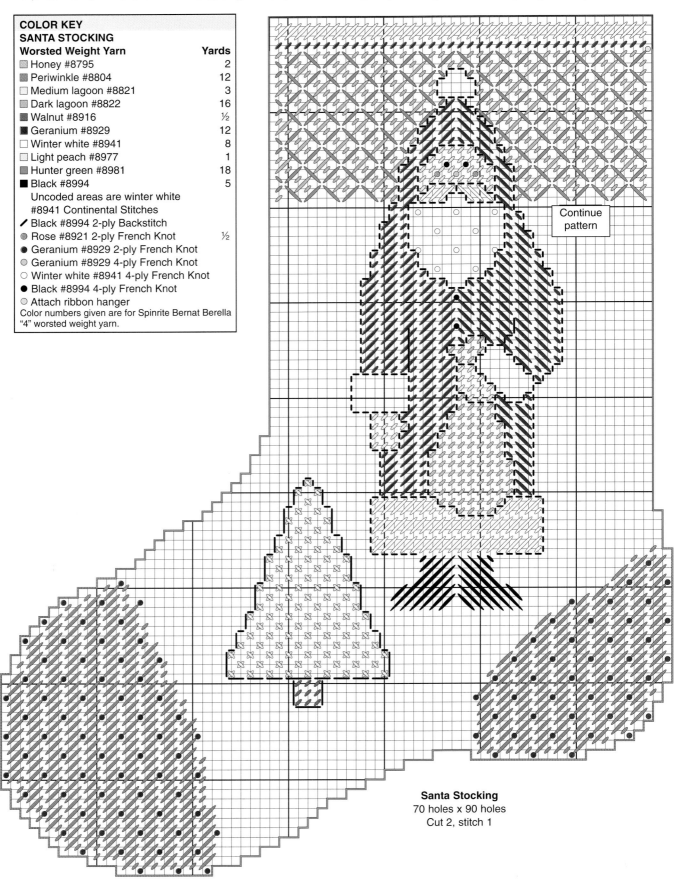

Continue pattern

Santa Stocking
70 holes x 90 holes
Cut 2, stitch 1

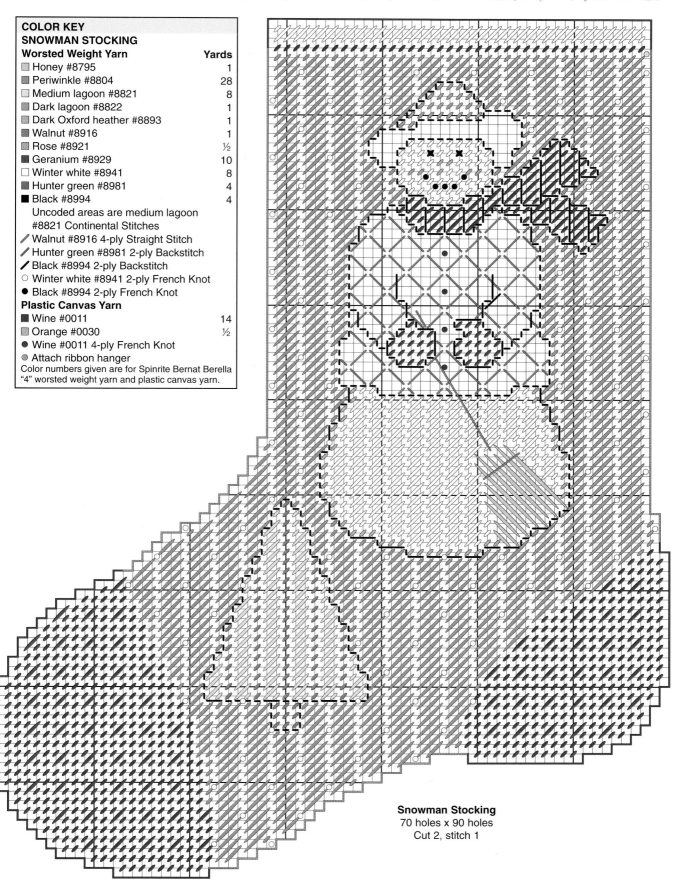

COLOR KEY
SNOWMAN STOCKING

Worsted Weight Yarn	Yards
☐ Honey #8795	1
▨ Periwinkle #8804	28
☐ Medium lagoon #8821	8
▨ Dark lagoon #8822	1
▨ Dark Oxford heather #8893	1
▧ Walnut #8916	1
▧ Rose #8921	½
■ Geranium #8929	10
☐ Winter white #8941	8
▨ Hunter green #8981	4
■ Black #8994	4

Uncoded areas are medium lagoon #8821 Continental Stitches

◢ Walnut #8916 4-ply Straight Stitch
◢ Hunter green #8981 2-ply Backstitch
◢ Black #8994 2-ply Backstitch
○ Winter white #8941 2-ply French Knot
● Black #8994 2-ply French Knot

Plastic Canvas Yarn
■ Wine #0011	14
▨ Orange #0030	½

● Wine #0011 4-ply French Knot
◉ Attach ribbon hanger

Color numbers given are for Spinrite Bernat Berella "4" worsted weight yarn and plastic canvas yarn.

Snowman Stocking
70 holes x 90 holes
Cut 2, stitch 1

COLOR KEY
ANGEL STOCKING

Worsted Weight Yarn	**Yards**
▨ Periwinkle #8804	6
☐ Medium lagoon #8821	8
▦ Dark lagoon #8822	10
▢ Light tapestry gold #8886	1
▨ Walnut #8916	½
■ Geranium #8929	26
☐ Winter white #8941	12
▢ Light peach #8977	1
▨ Hunter green #8981	3
Uncoded areas are midnight	
#8805 Continental Stitches	7
⁄ Dark lagoon #8822 2-ply Backstitch	
⁄ Black #8994 2-ply Backstitch	4
● Walnut #8916 2-ply French Knot	
○ Rose #8921 2-ply French Knot	½
● Geranium #8929 2-ply French Knot	
● Black #8994 4-ply French Knot	
Plastic Canvas Yarn	
● Wine #0011 2-ply French Knot	3
○ Thread yarn for hair bow	
○ Attach ribbon hanger	

Color numbers given are for Spinrite Bernat Berella
"4" worsted weight yarn and plastic canvas yarn.

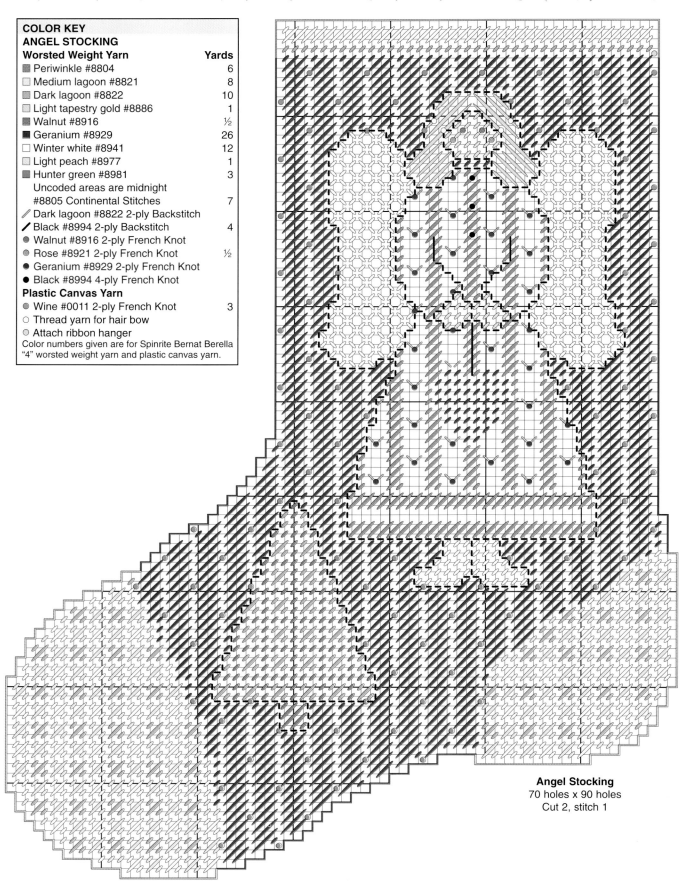

Angel Stocking
70 holes x 90 holes
Cut 2, stitch 1

Handy Stocking Hangers

Two festive shelf-sitting stocking hangers are as practical as they are decorative!

Joy Blocks

Skill Level
Intermediate

Materials
- 2⅓ sheets 7-count plastic canvas
- Plastic canvas yarn as listed in color key
- Stuffing pellets
- 1¼" drapery hook
- Hot-glue gun or craft glue

Instructions

1. Cut block pieces, one holder base and one holder tab from plastic canvas according to graphs (pages 100 and 101). Cut three 21-hole x 15-hole pieces for block bottoms. Block bottoms and two block sides (right side of "O" and left side of "Y") will remain unstitched.

2. Stitch pieces following graphs. With white, Whipstitch tab to base between blue dots, then Overcast remaining tab and base edges.

3. Using red through step 4, for each block, Whipstitch block front and back to two block sides, remembering

to use one unstitched side for each of blocks "O" and "Y" as stated in step 1.

4. Whipstitch tops and unstitched bottoms to each block, filling blocks "O" and "Y" with pellets before closing.

5. Glue unstitched sides of "O" and "Y" blocks together. Center and glue the "J" block on top of the "O" and "Y" blocks.

6. Center and glue assembled blocks to base. Insert drapery hook on tab between Scotch Stitches.

Sleigh

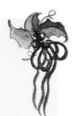

Skill Level

Intermediate

Materials

- 2⅓ sheets 7-count plastic canvas
- Plastic canvas yarn as listed in color key
- 1¼" drapery hook
- Candy
- Hot-glue gun or craft glue

Instructions

1. Cut sleigh pieces, one holder base and one holder tab from plastic canvas according to graphs (pages 102 and 103). Cut one 25-hole x 15-hole piece for sleigh bottom. Sleigh bottom will remain unstitched.

2. Stitch pieces following graphs, reversing one runner before stitching. With white, Whipstitch tab to base between blue dots, then Overcast remaining tab and base edges.

3. With green, Whipstitch back and front to short edges of sleigh bottom. With yellow and with right sides facing, Whipstitch runners to runners on sleigh.

4. With green, Whipstitch front and back to sleigh sides. Whipstitch bottom to sleigh sides where indicated on side graphs. Overcast all remaining edges with green.

5. Center and glue sleigh to holder base. Fill sleigh with candy.

Designed by Karen McDanel

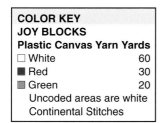

COLOR KEY
JOY BLOCKS
Plastic Canvas Yarn Yards
☐ White   60
■ Red   30
▨ Green   20
  Uncoded areas are white
  Continental Stitches

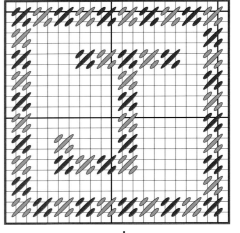

J
21 holes x 21 holes
Cut 1

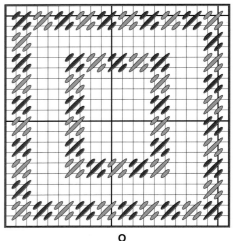

O
21 holes x 21 holes
Cut 1

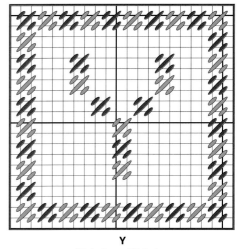

Y
21 holes x 21 holes
Cut 1

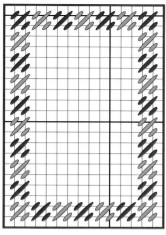

Block Side
15 holes x 21 holes
Cut 6, stitch 4

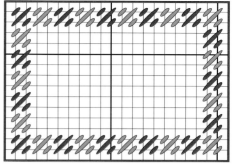

Block Top
21 holes x 15 holes
Cut 3

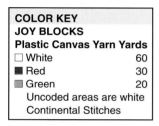

COLOR KEY
JOY BLOCKS
Plastic Canvas Yarn Yards
☐ White 60
■ Red 30
▨ Green 20
Uncoded areas are white
Continental Stitches

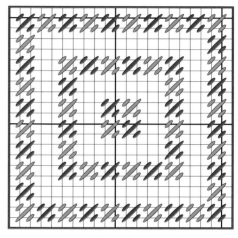

Block Back
21 holes x 21 holes
Cut 3

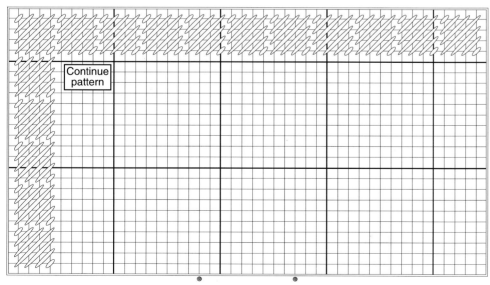

Continue
pattern

Stocking Holder Base
45 holes x 25 holes
Cut 1 for each holder

Stocking Holder Tab
9 holes x 13 holes
Cut 1 for each holder

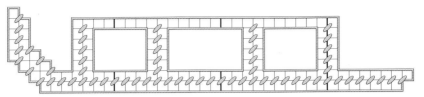

Sleigh Runner
38 holes x 8 holes
Cut 2, reverse 1

COLOR KEY	
SLEIGH	
Plastic Canvas Yarn	**Yards**
☐ White	55
▨ Green	25
■ Red	19
▨ Yellow	12
— Whipstitch to sleigh bottom	

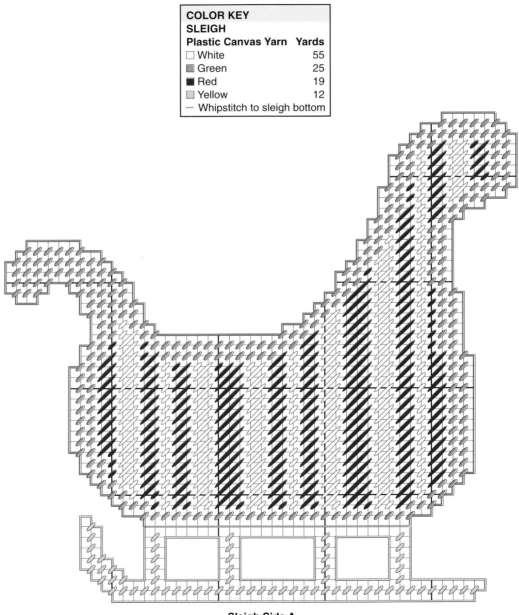

Sleigh Side A
48 holes x 46 holes
Cut 1

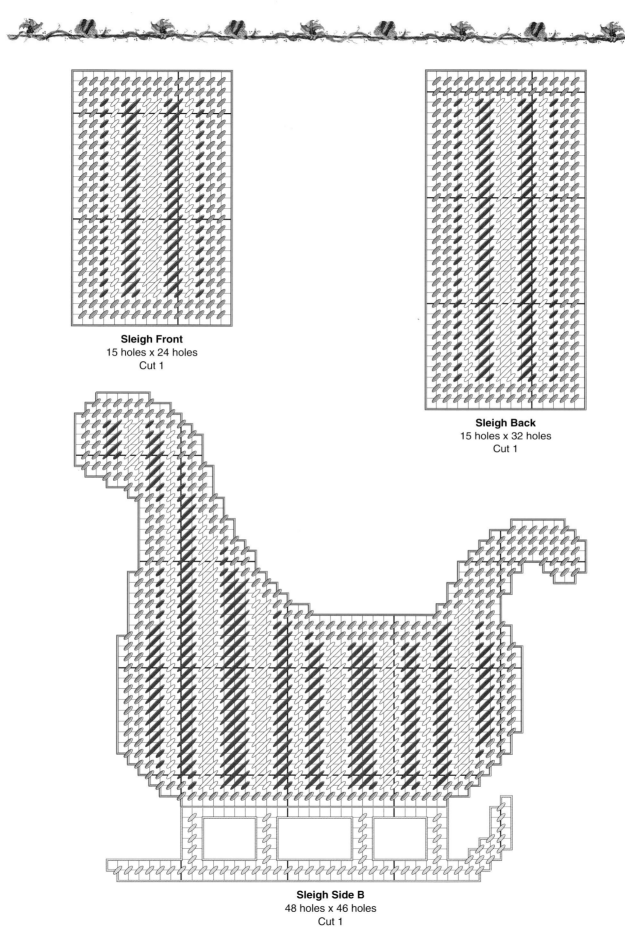

Sleigh Front
15 holes x 24 holes
Cut 1

Sleigh Back
15 holes x 32 holes
Cut 1

Sleigh Side B
48 holes x 46 holes
Cut 1

Mock-Knit Stockings

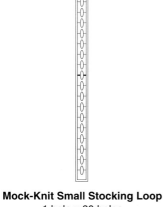

Friends and family won't believe these attractive stockings are actually plastic canvas! A clever stitch and argyle pattern makes them appear to be knit!

Skill Level
Beginner

Materials
- 3 sheets 7-count plastic canvas
- Uniek Needloft plastic canvas yarn as listed in color key
- Uniek Needloft Craft Cord as listed in color key
- #16 tapestry needle
- Hot-glue gun

COLOR KEY	
Plastic Canvas Yarn	**Yards**
■ Christmas red #02	194
■ Christmas green #28	36
□ White #41	78
Metallic Craft Cord	
□ Gold #01	24
Color numbers given are for Uniek Needloft plastic canvas yarn and craft cord.	

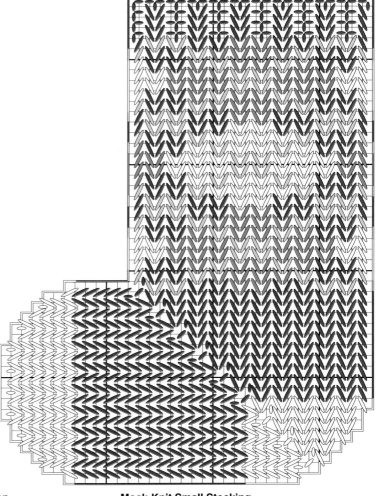

Mock-Knit Small Stocking Loop
1 hole x 20 holes
Cut 1

Mock-Knit Large Stocking Loop
1 hole x 25 holes
Cut 1

Mock-Knit Small Stocking
35 holes x 46 holes
Cut 2, reverse 1

Instructions

1. Cut plastic canvas according to graphs (also see page 106).

2. Stitch pieces following graphs, reversing one large and one small stocking before stitching.

3. Overcast loops with white and top edges of stockings with Christmas red. With wrong sides together, Whipstitch small stockings together and large stockings together with adjacent colors.

4. Fold loops in half and glue ends in top back corner of corresponding stocking.

Designed by Angie Arickx

COLOR KEY

Plastic Canvas Yarn	Yards
■ Christmas red #02	194
▨ Christmas green #28	36
□ White #41	78
Metallic Craft Cord	
□ Gold #01	24

Color numbers given are for Uniek
Needloft plastic canvas yarn and
craft cord.

Mock-Knit Large Stocking
70 holes x 90 holes
Cut 2, reverse 1

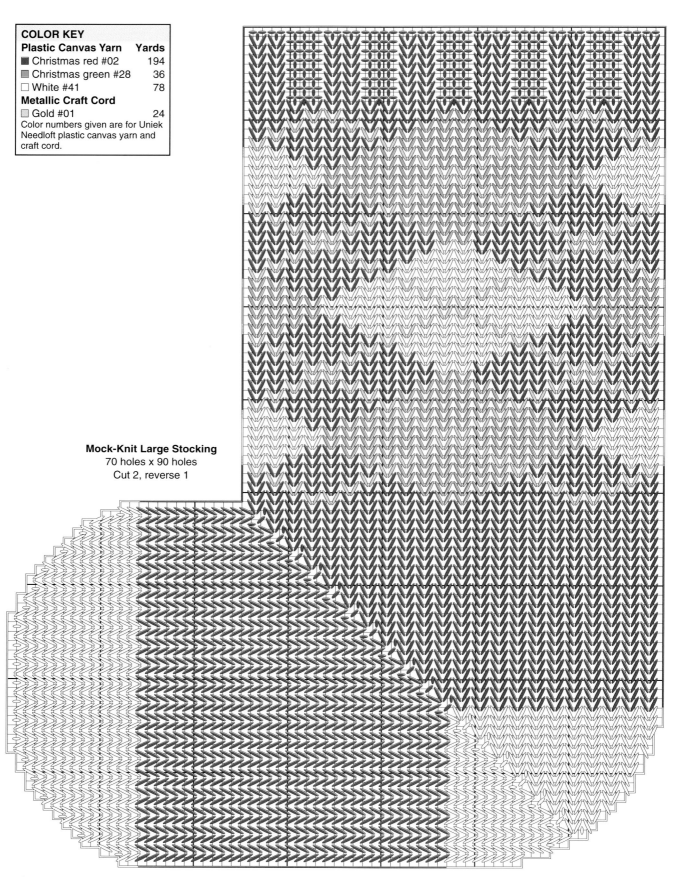

Poinsettia Tissue Topper

Stitch this eye-catching tissue box cover adorned with vibrant red and pink poinsettias. A bright bow adds a festive touch! See the photo on page 109.

Skill Level
Advanced

Materials
- 2 sheets 7-count plastic canvas
- Worsted weight yarn as listed in color key
- #3 pearl cotton as listed in color key

Instructions

1. Cut plastic canvas according to graphs (also see page 108).

2. Stitch pieces following graphs. Over completed background stitching, work Backstitches first, then French Knots, combining 2 plies pale lime green and 2 plies grenadine for French Knots.

3. Using white through step 4, Overcast bottom edges of sides. For bows, Overcast around side edges and short edge without dots. With right sides facing up, Whipstitch bow edges to inside edges of top where indicated on graph with blue dots. Overcast remaining inside edges of top. Turn bows under, placing bow edges one row behind inside edges; tack to top piece.

4. Whipstitch sides together, alternating sides A with sides B. Whipstitch sides to top.

Designed by Conn Baker Gibney

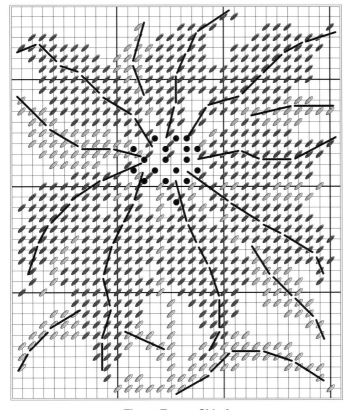

Tissue Topper Side A
31 holes x 37 holes
Cut 2

COLOR KEY	
Worsted Weight Yarn	**Yards**
■ Red	20
▨ Grenadine	18
▨ Emerald green	12
Uncoded areas are white Continental Stitches	25
⁄ White Overcasting and Whipstitching	
● Pale lime green and grenadine French Knots	1
#3 Pearl Cotton	
⁄ Garnet Backstitch	9

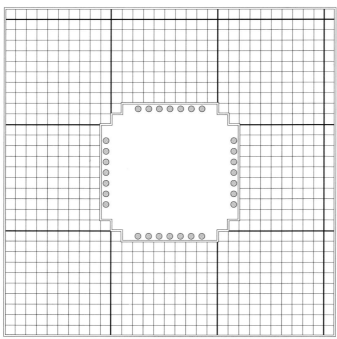

Tissue Topper Top
31 holes x 31 holes
Cut 1

COLOR KEY	
Worsted Weight Yarn	**Yards**
■ Red	20
▨ Grenadine	18
▨ Emerald green	12
Uncoded areas are white	
Continental Stitches	25
⁄ White Overcasting	
and Whipstitching	
● Pale lime green and	
grenadine French Knots	1
#3 Pearl Cotton	
⁄ Garnet Backstitch	9

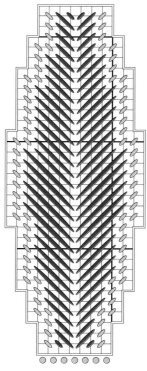

Tissue Topper Bow
13 holes x 33 holes
Cut 4

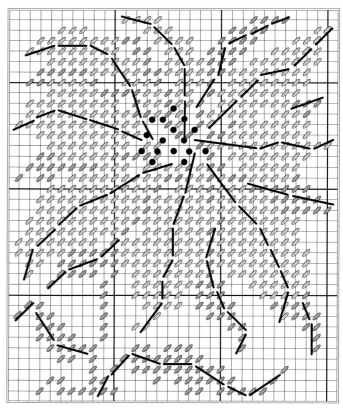

Tissue Topper Side B
31 holes x 37 holes
Cut 2

Christmas Goose
Centerpiece

Instructions begin on page 112

Festive Decor

Christmas Goose Centerpiece

Add a special touch to Christmas dinner by displaying this lovely goose centerpiece adorned with pine, holly, fruit and festive ribbon. See the photo on page 110.

Skill Level
Beginner

Materials
- 2 sheets 7-count Darice Ultra Stiff plastic canvas
- Spinrite plastic canvas yarn as listed in color key
- 12" ⅞"-wide plaid ribbon
- Several fruit and berry picks
- Scraps artificial evergreen with pinecones
- Small amount polyester fiberfill
- Low-temperature glue gun

Cutting & Stitching
1. Cut plastic canvas according to graphs.

2. Stitch pieces following graphs, reversing one goose and one wing before stitching. Overcast wings with white and base with clover.

3. Following graph, Whipstitch wrong sides of goose together, beginning at the head and stuffing lightly while Whipstitching body together. Whipstitch goose bottom to bottom edges of goose.

4. Using photo as a guide throughout, center and glue goose to base. Glue wings to sides of goose. Arrange and glue fruit, berries, evergreen and pinecones around base of goose as desired.

5. Tie ribbon in a bow around base of neck. Glue berries as desired to center of bow.

Designed by Celia Lange Designs

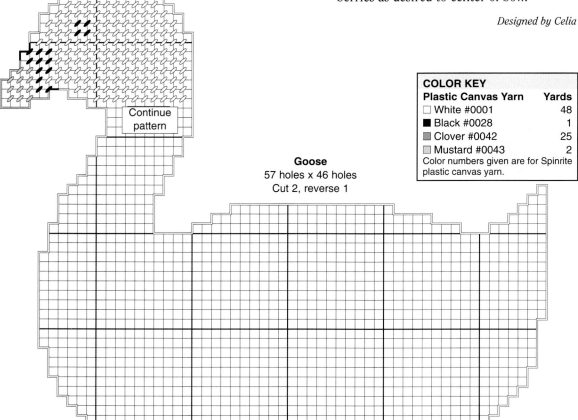

Continue pattern

Goose
57 holes x 46 holes
Cut 2, reverse 1

COLOR KEY	
Plastic Canvas Yarn	**Yards**
☐ White #0001	48
■ Black #0028	1
▩ Clover #0042	25
▨ Mustard #0043	2
Color numbers given are for Spinrite plastic canvas yarn.	

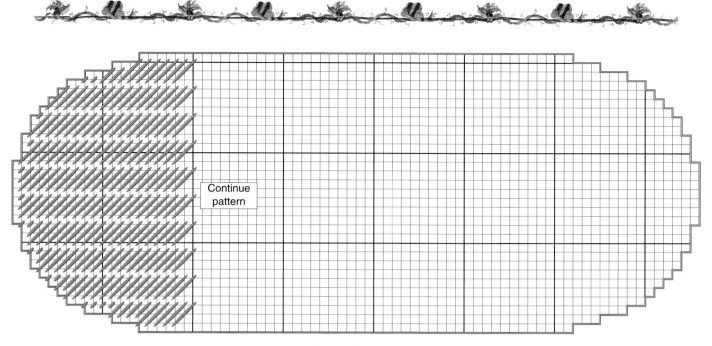

Centerpiece Base
76 holes x 31 holes
Cut 1

Continue
pattern

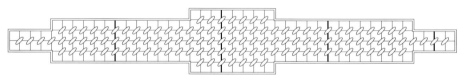

Goose Bottom
42 holes x 6 holes
Cut 1

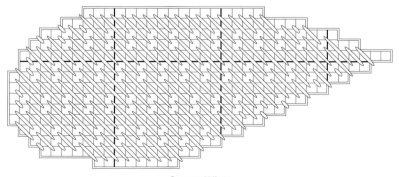

Goose Wing
36 holes x 15 holes
Cut 2, reverse 1

Gingerbread Wreath

Nothing smells quite so good on Christmas Eve as warm wassail and gingerbread cookies! Stitch this engaging wreath to welcome family and friends to your Christmas Eve carol-singing party!

Skill Level
Beginner

Materials
- 1 sheet 7-count plastic canvas
- Uniek Needloft plastic canvas yarn as listed in color key
- #16 tapestry needle
- Purchased Christmas wreath (sample used 15" wreath)
- Hot-glue gun

Instructions

1. Cut plastic canvas according to graphs (also see page 116).

2. Continental Stitch pieces following graphs, working Backstitches over completed background stitching. Overcast hearts with maple. Overcast gingerbread Santa with maple, white and red, following graph.

3. Using photo as a guide, glue pieces to wreath, placing gingerbread Santa on the left. Attach heart pieces clockwise so message reads "All hearts come home for Christmas," ending with the double heart on the bottom.

Designed by Angie Arickx

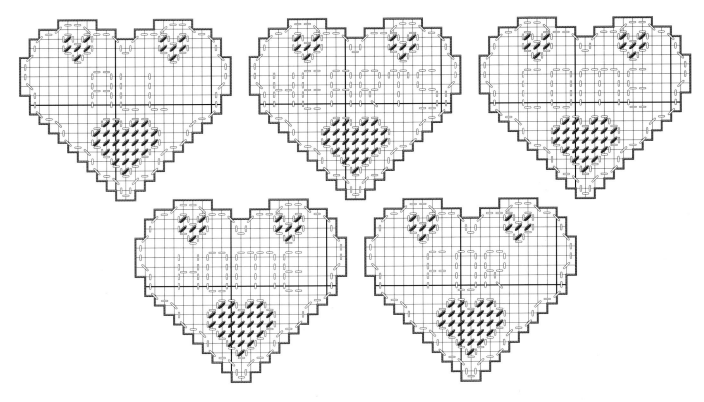

Single Hearts
22 holes x 19 holes
Cut 1 each

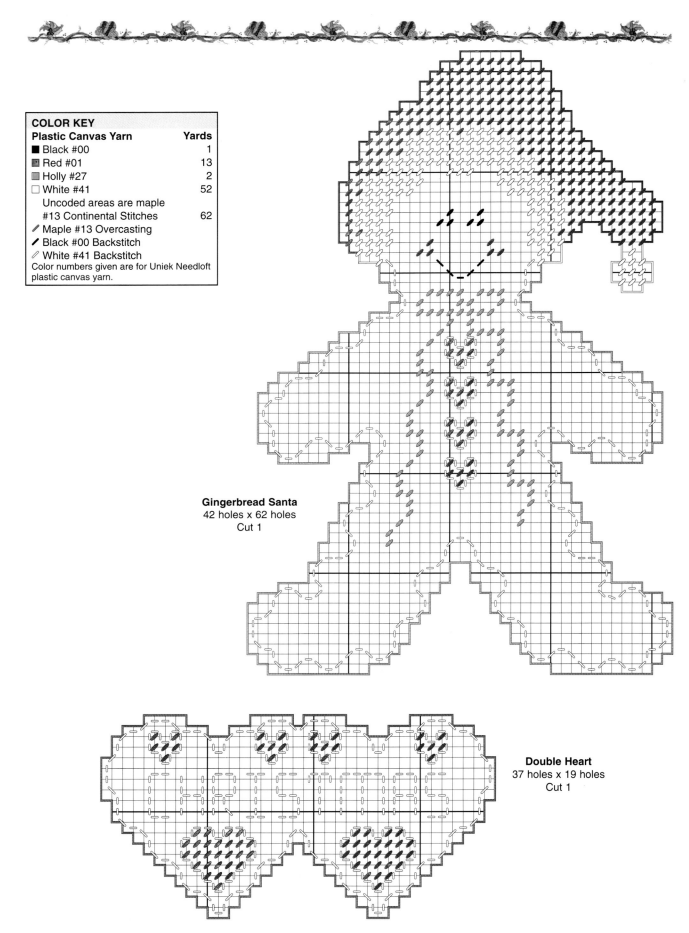

COLOR KEY

Plastic Canvas Yarn	Yards
■ Black #00	1
▨ Red #01	13
▨ Holly #27	2
□ White #41	52
Uncoded areas are maple #13 Continental Stitches	62
╱ Maple #13 Overcasting	
╱ Black #00 Backstitch	
╱ White #41 Backstitch	

Color numbers given are for Uniek Needloft plastic canvas yarn.

Gingerbread Santa
42 holes x 62 holes
Cut 1

Double Heart
37 holes x 19 holes
Cut 1

Beary Christmas

Welcome your holiday guests into your home with this cheerful sign hand-stitched with love and hospitality!

Skill Level
Intermediate

Materials
- 3 sheets 7-count plastic canvas
- Uniek Needloft plastic canvas yarn as listed in color key
- #16 tapestry needle
- 6 (10.5mm x 10mm) ruby heart cabochons by The Beadery
- 2 (20mm) black round cabochons by The Beadery
- 3 (¾") gold jingle bells
- 30" ⅜"-wide red with white polka dot grosgrain ribbon
- 9" ¼"-wide white satin ribbon
- Sawtooth hanger
- Hot-glue gun

Cutting & Stitching
1. Cut plastic canvas according to graphs (also see pages 119–121). Letters, head back, hat back and sign back will remain unstitched.

2. Stitch pieces following graphs, stitching border on sign first, filling in center last. Work white Long Stitches for hat cuff, working two stitches per hole. Overcast letters, holly, muzzle, nose, paws and feet following graphs. Work Backstitches and Straight Stitches on muzzle, paws and leaves when background stitching and Overcasting are completed.

3. Overcast bottom edge of hat front with white. Whipstitch hat front to hat back around side and top edges with adjacent colors, leaving portion of top edge from dot to dot unstitched.

Continued on page 120

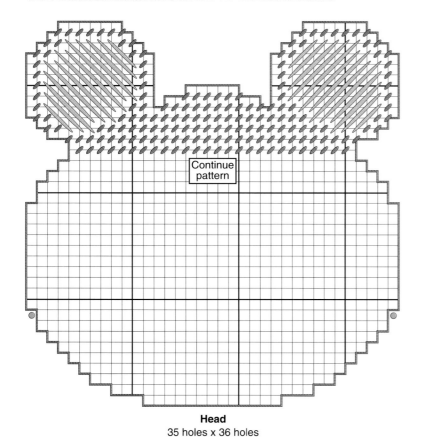

Head
35 holes x 36 holes
Cut 2, stitch 1

Continue pattern

Paw
15 holes x 12 holes
Cut 2

COLOR KEY	
Plastic Canvas Yarn	**Yards**
■ Black #00	2
■ Christmas red #02	24
▨ Maple #13	30
▨ Holly #27	16
▨ Beige #40	11
□ White #41	38
╱ Black #00 Backstitch and Straight Stitch	
╱ Holly #27 Straight Stitch	
Color numbers given are for Uniek Needloft plastic canvas yarn.	

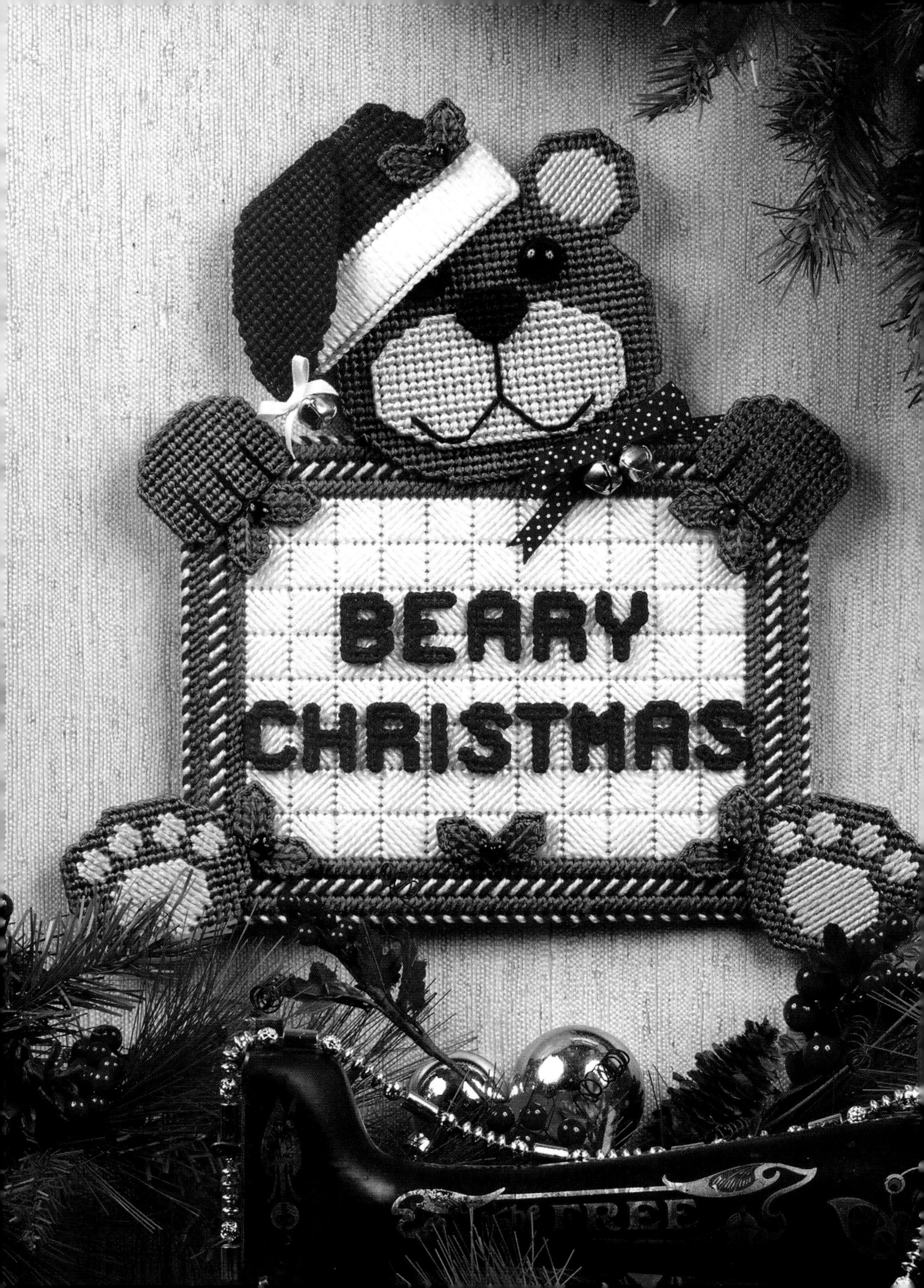
BEARY
CHRISTMAS

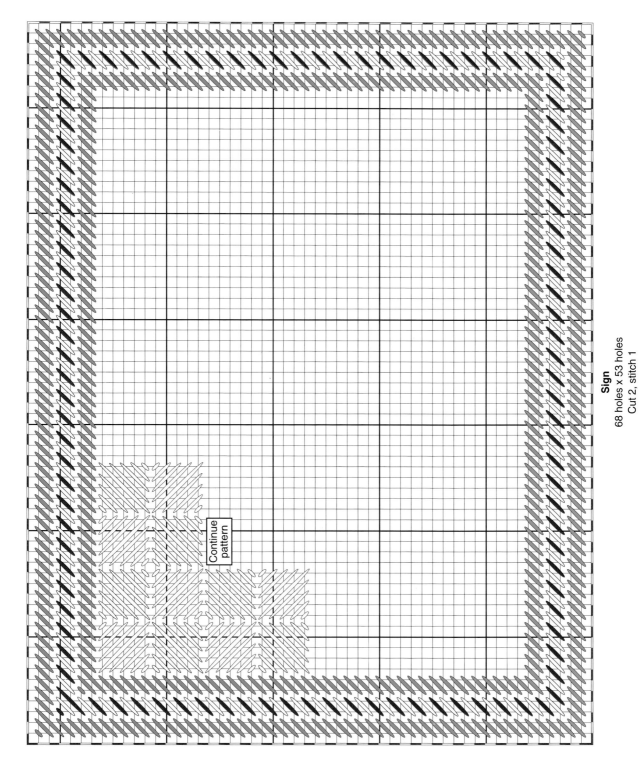

Sign
68 holes x 53 holes
Cut 2, stitch 1

Continue pattern

Nose
7 holes x 5 holes
Cut 1

Holly Leaf
5 holes x 5 holes
Cut 12

Festive Decor   119

4. Using Christmas red throughout, Overcast around side and bottom edges of hat dangle. With wrong side of hat dangle on right side of hat, Whipstitch top edge of hat dangle to unstitched portion of top edges on hat front and back.

5. Using maple throughout, Overcast bottom edge of head front and back from dot to dot. Whipstitch remaining edges of head front to head back.

6. Following graph, Whipstitch sign front to sign back, alternating Christmas red with white.

Assembly

1. Using photo as a guide throughout assembly, glue letters to center section of sign. Glue 10 holly leaves in clusters of two to the four corners of center section and to center bottom edge of center section on sign. Glue one heart cabochon to each holly leaf cluster where leaves are joined together.

2. Glue muzzle to head, then glue nose to center top edge of muzzle. Glue black cabochons for eyes above muzzle. Glue front of head to center top of sign, tilting slightly to the left. With maple, neatly tack bottom edge of head back to sign back.

3. Slip hat opening over ear on left side of head. Glue hat front to head front. With white, neatly tack bottom edge of hat back to head back.

4. Glue two holly leaves to right side of hat above cuff. Glue heart cabochon to holly leaves as in step 1. Tie white ribbon in a bow; trim ends. Glue bow to tip of hat dangle. Glue one jingle bell directly under bow.

5. Glue paws to top corners of sign and feet to bottom corners of sign. Sew or glue sawtooth hanger to back of

head just above bottom edge.

6. Cut polka dot ribbon into the following lengths: one 1", two 3", one 4", one 5", one 6" and one 7". Cut an inverted "V" into one end of each 3" length.

7. Glue ends of 4" length together, forming a circle. Repeat with the 5", 6" and 7" lengths. Flatten circles into loops and place on top of each other in graduated sizes, with the largest on bottom and the smallest on top. Wrap center of loops with 1" ribbon, forming a bow; glue on backside to secure. Glue 3" lengths to back of bow for tails.

8. Glue completed bow to sign at bottom right side of face. Glue remaining two jingle bells directly under center of bow.

Designed by Vicki Blizzard

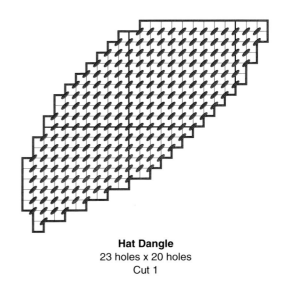

Hat Dangle
23 holes x 20 holes
Cut 1

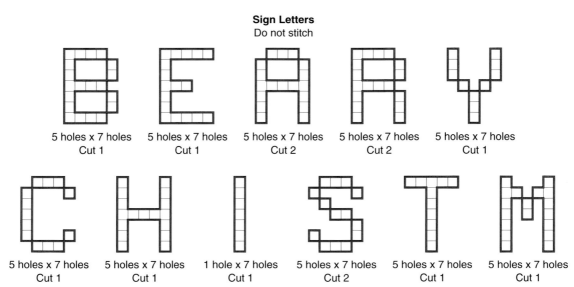

Sign Letters
Do not stitch

5 holes x 7 holes
Cut 1

5 holes x 7 holes
Cut 1

5 holes x 7 holes
Cut 2

5 holes x 7 holes
Cut 2

5 holes x 7 holes
Cut 1

5 holes x 7 holes
Cut 1

5 holes x 7 holes
Cut 1

1 hole x 7 holes
Cut 1

5 holes x 7 holes
Cut 2

5 holes x 7 holes
Cut 1

5 holes x 7 holes
Cut 1

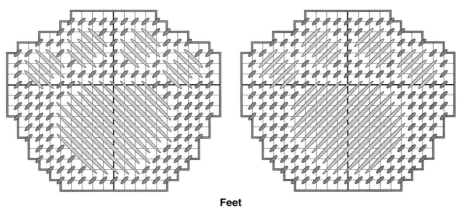

Feet
20 holes x 17 holes
Cut 1 each

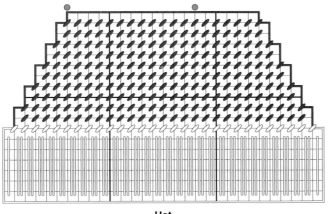

Hat
30 holes x 18 holes
Cut 2, stitch 1

COLOR KEY

Plastic Canvas Yarn	Yards
■ Black #00	2
■ Christmas red #02	24
■ Maple #13	30
■ Holly #27	16
■ Beige #40	11
□ White #41	38
╱ Black #00 Backstitch and Straight Stitch	
╱ Holly #27 Straight Stitch	

Color numbers given are for Uniek Needloft plastic canvas yarn.

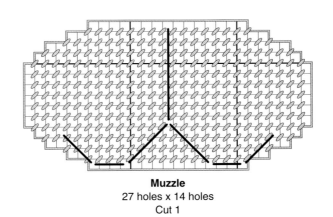

Muzzle
27 holes x 14 holes
Cut 1

Whimsical Elf Doorstop

This delightful doorstop—bursting with all the personality of one of Santa's elves—will bring a smile to everyone's face while serving as a practical decoration!

Skill Level
Advanced beginner

Materials
- 1½ sheets 7-count plastic canvas
- Uniek Needloft plastic canvas yarn as listed in color key
- DMC #3 pearl cotton as listed in color key
- #16 tapestry needle
- #18 tapestry needle
- Brick
- Hot-glue gun

Instructions
1. Cut plastic canvas according to graphs. Cut one 51-hole x 26-hole piece for doorstop back, one 51-hole x

16-hole piece for doorstop top and two 16-hole x 26-hole pieces for doorstop sides.

2. Continental Stitch pieces following graphs, leaving row marked with blue on front unstitched at this time. With tan, Continental Stitch back, top and sides. Backstitch nose and mouth with pearl cotton over completed background stitching.

3. Overcast elf, elf feet and top part of legs and body following graphs.

4. Using tan throughout, Overcast bottom edges of front, sides and back. Whipstitch top to unworked bar on front, then Whipstitch top to top edges of back and sides. Whipstitch sides to front and back.

5. Center and glue elf to front so elf's chin is three rows above the top "R" in "MERRY." Place stitched doorstop over brick.

Designed by Angie Arickx

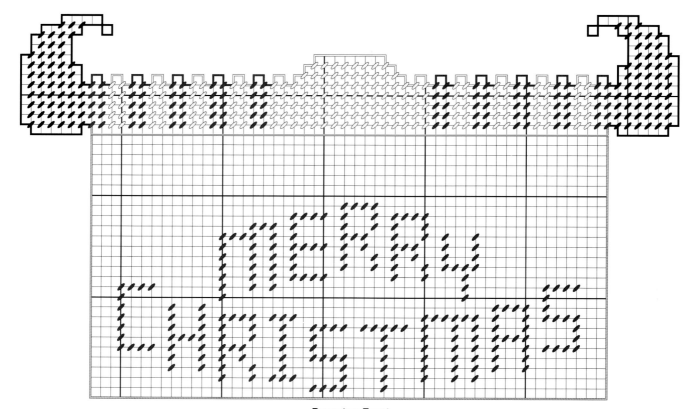

Doorstop Front
65 holes x 38 holes
Cut 1

COLOR KEY

Plastic Canvas Yarn	Yards
■ Black #00	4
▨ Lavender #05	1
▨ Maple #13	1
▥ Forest #29	7
▨ Royal #32	1
▢ Eggshell #39	7
▢ White #41	1
■ Crimson #42	8
Uncoded areas on front are tan #18 Continental Stitches	80
Uncoded areas on elf are flesh tone #57 Continental Stitches	3
⟋ Tan #18 Overcasting and Whipstitching	
⟋ Flesh tone #57 Overcasting	
⟋ Whipstitch to top	
#3 Pearl Cotton	
⟋ Bronze #300 Backstitch	1

Color numbers given are for Uniek Needloft plastic canvas yarn and DMC #3 pearl cotton.

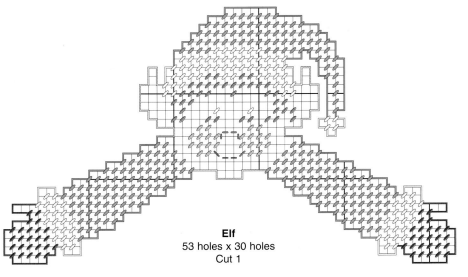

Elf
53 holes x 30 holes
Cut 1

Happy Ho-Ho Days

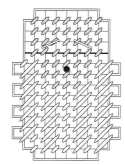

Whether it's the postman dropping off the mail, or a group of youngsters singing carols, all guests who come to your front door will appreciate and enjoy this happy holidays sign.

Skill Level
Beginner

Materials
- 9" plastic canvas radial circle by Darice
- 1 sheet 7-count plastic canvas
- Spinrite plastic canvas yarn as listed in color key
- Kreinik Medium (#16) Braid as listed in color key
- #16 tapestry needle
- 16 (10.5mm x 10mm) ruby heart cabochons by The Beadery
- 6 (5mm) black round cabochons by The Beadery
- 3 (6mm) red round beads by The Beadery
- 6 (⅝") gold jingle bells
- 3 (¼") white pompons
- 1½ yards ⅜"-wide gold ribbon
- 9" x 12" sheet white felt
- Sewing needle and clear thread
- Sawtooth hanger
- Hot-glue gun

Cutting & Stitching
1. Cut plastic canvas according to graphs (also see page 126). Using circle and three Santa heads as templates, cut felt slightly smaller than each piece.

2. Using almond through step 4, Straight Stitch circle over three bars from the first outside row of holes to the fourth row of holes, using two stitches per hole as necessary in the fourth row of holes.

3. Moving toward the center, Straight Stitch around circle over three bars from the fourth row of holes to the seventh row of holes, using two stitches per hole in the seventh row of holes as necessary.

4. Repeat seven more times, stitching around circle over three bars each time and using two stitches per hole as necessary on the inside row of holes. Finish piece by Straight Stitching across the center, covering remaining canvas. Overcast outside edge of circle.

5. Stitch leaves and Santa pieces following graphs. Work white Straight Stitches for eyebrows on Santa heads over completed background stitching. Overcast heads and mustaches with white and holly leaves with brisk green.

6. For hats and hat dangles, Overcast around side and bottom edges with adjacent colors. With wrong side of hat dangles on right side of corresponding hats, Whipstitch top edges together with adjacent colors.

7. Overcast letters with wine. Work gold braid embroidery when Overcasting is completed.

Assembly
1. Glue felt to backside of circle and Santa heads.

2. Using photo as a guide throughout assembly, glue leaves in 15 clusters of three around circle edge. ***Note: There will be three leaves left over.*** Glue one heart cabochon to the center of each three-leaf cluster.

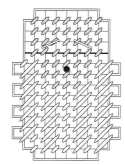

Left Santa Head
10 holes x 14 holes
Cut 1

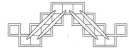

Left Santa Mustache
11 holes x 4 holes
Cut 1

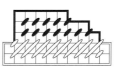

Left Santa Hat
10 holes x 5 holes
Cut 1

Left Santa Hat Dangle
5 holes x 8 holes
Cut 1

3. Glue remaining three leaves in a cluster approximately ¾" from holly leaves at center top of circle. Glue remaining heart cabochon to center of this cluster.

4. Cut an 8" length of gold ribbon and tie in a bow. Cut an inverted "V" in the end of each tail. Glue bow in ¾" space between holly leaves at top of circle.

5. Cut remaining ribbon into three equal lengths. Holding ribbon together, fold in half and stitch center point to bottom back of circle with clear thread. Tie a gold jingle bell to each ribbon end, making ribbon different lengths. Trim ends as necessary.

6. Using clear thread, sew round red beads for noses to Santa faces where indicated on graphs. For eyes, glue black cabochons to heads under eyebrows.

7. Glue mustaches to corresponding heads under noses. Glue pompons to tips of hat dangles.

8. Center and glue letters to circle. Glue Santas with corresponding hats to circle under letters. Glue sawtooth hanger to center top backside of circle.

Designed by Vicki Blizzard

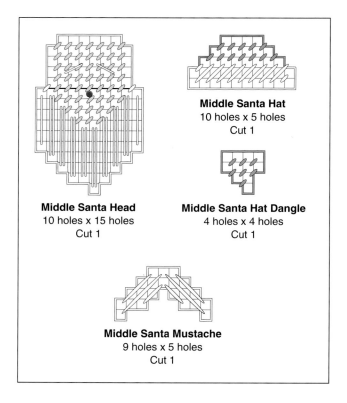

Middle Santa Head
10 holes x 15 holes
Cut 1

Middle Santa Hat
10 holes x 5 holes
Cut 1

Middle Santa Hat Dangle
4 holes x 4 holes
Cut 1

Middle Santa Mustache
9 holes x 5 holes
Cut 1

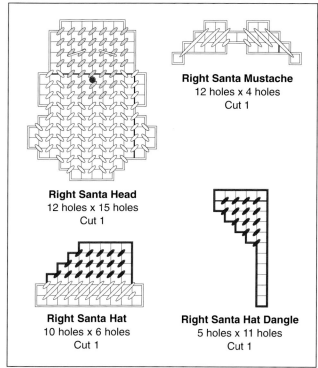

Right Santa Mustache
12 holes x 4 holes
Cut 1

Right Santa Head
12 holes x 15 holes
Cut 1

Right Santa Hat
10 holes x 6 holes
Cut 1

Right Santa Hat Dangle
5 holes x 11 holes
Cut 1

Holly Leaf
5 holes x 7 holes
Cut 48

COLOR KEY	
Plastic Canvas Yarn	**Yards**
☐ White #0001	10
☐ Peach #0007	3
■ Wine #0011	10
■ Brisk green #0027	31
Almond #0056	35
✐ White #0001 Straight Stitch	
Medium (#16) Braid	
✐ Gold #002HL Backstitch and Straight Stitch	
● Attach red bead	
Color numbers given are for Spinrite plastic canvas yarn and Kreinik Medium (#16) Braid.	

Letters
5 holes x 7 holes

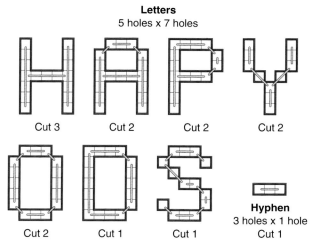

Cut 3   Cut 2   Cut 2   Cut 2

Cut 2   Cut 1   Cut 1

Hyphen
3 holes x 1 hole
Cut 1

Santa Magnet

Tack up your holiday shopping list or important "things-to-do" list with this colorful, three-dimensional magnet!

Skill Level
Beginner

Materials
- 1 sheet 7-count plastic canvas
- Worsted weight yarn as listed in color key
- ½" white sparkle craft pompon
- 21 (5mm) faceted beads in various colors
- Sewing needle and green thread
- 3 (1") lengths magnetic strip
- Hot-glue gun

Instructions

1. Cut plastic canvas according to graphs (page 128).

2. Stitch pieces following graphs, leaving blue area on hands unstitched. Work embroidery over completed background stitching.

3. Overcast mustache with white and Santa with adjacent colors. Overcast hands and star with adjacent colors, leaving outside edges on hands from dot to dot unstitched. With gold yarn, Whipstitch outside edges of hands to Santa where indicated on graph.

4. With white yarn, tack mustache to face under nose. With sewing needle and green thread, attach beads to tree where desired.

5. Glue pompon to top of Santa's hat. Glue magnetic strips to back of Santa.

Designed by Kristine Loffredo

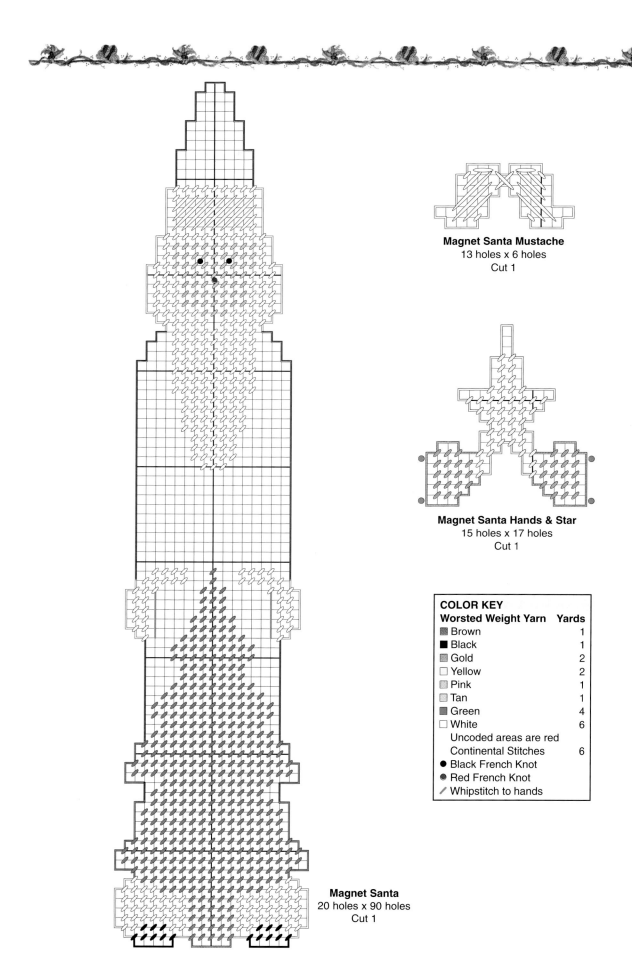

Magnet Santa Mustache
13 holes x 6 holes
Cut 1

Magnet Santa Hands & Star
15 holes x 17 holes
Cut 1

COLOR KEY

Worsted Weight Yarn	Yards
▨ Brown	1
■ Black	1
▨ Gold	2
□ Yellow	2
▨ Pink	1
▨ Tan	1
▨ Green	4
□ White	6
Uncoded areas are red Continental Stitches	6
● Black French Knot	
● Red French Knot	
╱ Whipstitch to hands	

Magnet Santa
20 holes x 90 holes
Cut 1

I ♥ Snowmen

If you're not up to building a snowman with the kids, why not stitch a trio of cheerful snowmen who won't melt away!

Skill Level
Beginner

Materials
- ⅔ sheet 7-count plastic canvas
- Uniek Needloft plastic canvas yarn as listed in color key
- #3 pearl cotton: 2 yards white and as listed in color key
- 2 yards ⅛"-wide red satin ribbon
- 4 (⅞") yellow-orange buttons
- 2 (⅞") red buttons

Instructions
1. Cut plastic canvas according to graph (page 130).

2. Continental Stitch front following graph. Work black pearl cotton French Knots over completed background stitching. Back will remain unstitched.

3. Using photo as a guide, sew buttons to front with white pearl cotton. With mermaid, Whipstitch front and back together.

4. For hanger, cut ribbon in half. Thread one half through left hole and one through right hole where indicated on graph. Make ends even; tie both lengths together in a bow (see photo).

Designed by Michele Wilcox

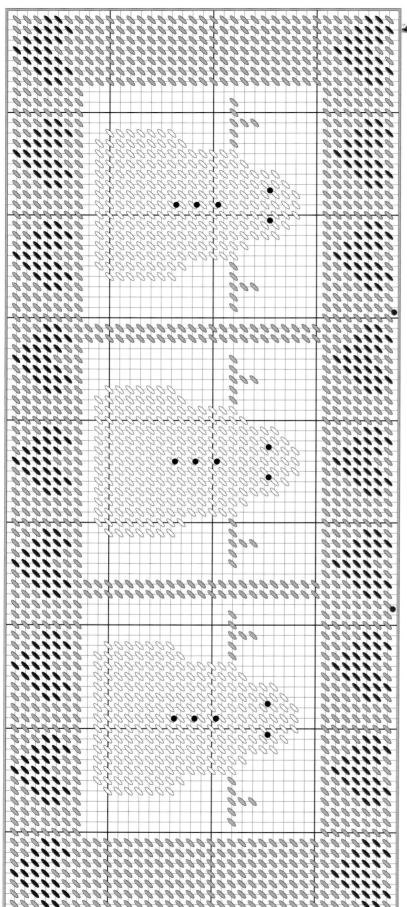

I Love Snowmen
88 holes x 38 holes
Cut 2, stitch 1

Santa & Snowman Surprise Boxes

Give two gifts in one by tucking a loved one's holiday present inside one of these festive gift boxes, created with a touch of personality!

Santa

Skill Level
Intermediate

Materials
- 2 (6") plastic canvas heart shapes by Uniek
- ½ sheet 7-count plastic canvas
- Spinrite plastic canvas yarn as listed in color key
- Kreinik Medium (#16) Braid as listed in color key
- WYndemasters GlissenGloss Estaz fuzzy garland fiber by Madeira as listed in color key
- #16 tapestry needle
- 2 (5mm) black round cabochons by The Beadery
- 10 (4mm) gold round beads by The Beadery
- 6mm red round bead by The Beadery
- 6" square red felt
- Clear thread
- Hot-glue gun

Instructions

1. Cut plastic canvas according to graphs (pages 134–135). Trim one outside row of holes from one heart shape for box bottom, which will remain unstitched. Using box bottom as a template, cut felt to use for lid lining.

2. Stitch pieces following graphs, reversing two arm pieces before stitching. Overcast pompon with white. For pompon and white areas of Santa's hat, jacket and curves on lid top, stitch with white yarn first. Using 12" lengths, stitch fuzzy garland fiber over these white stitches, following Fig. 1, coming up at odd numbers and going down at even numbers.

3. Work gold braid Straight Stitches and Backstitches for belt buckle and jacket closures. Using 2 plies, Backstitch mouth with scarlet yarn and Straight Stitch eyebrows with white yarn. With clear thread, attach gold beads on jacket and red bead on face where indicated on graph. Glue black cabochons under eyebrows for eyes.

4. For beard, with white yarn, go down at first dot on graph, leaving a 1½" tail. Come up at second dot, then go back down in second dot, leaving a 1½" loop. Repeat for all beard dots, coming up in last dot, cutting yarn and leaving a 1½" tail. Cut loops, fray all ends and trim evenly to desired length.

5. For mustache, cut two 3½" lengths of white yarn. Thread ends of both lengths from back to front through holes indicated on graph; tie lengths together under nose. Fray ends and trim to desired length.

6. Using wine throughout, with right sides together, Whipstitch short edges on one end of box sides together. Bring sides around and with wrong sides together, Whipstitch remaining short edges together, forming a heart. Aligning points, Whipstitch bottom edges of box sides to box bottom, easing side pieces to fit around curves. Overcast top edges of box sides.

7. With right sides together, Whipstitch short edges on one end of lid sides together with wine; bring sides around and with wrong sides together, Whipstitch remaining short edges together, forming a heart. Aligning points, and following lid top graph, Whipstitch top edges of lid sides to lid top, easing side pieces to fit around curve. Overcast bottom edges of lid sides with wine. Glue red felt lining to wrong side of lid top.

8. With wrong sides together and matching edges, Whipstitch two arm pieces together with adjacent colors. Cut a 4" length of fuzzy garland fiber. Secure end on back of arm at cuff, then wrap three times around for fur. Glue end to back of arm. Repeat with remaining two arm pieces.

9. Using photo as guide, glue arms to jacket and pompon to tip of hat.

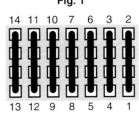

Fig. 1

Come up at odd numbers, go down at even numbers.

Snowman

Materials
- 2 (6") plastic canvas heart shapes by Uniek
- ½ sheet 7-count plastic canvas
- Spinrite plastic canvas yarn as listed in color key
- Kreinik Medium (#16) Braid as listed in color key
- Kreinik Fine (#8) Braid as listed in color key
- WYndemasters GlissenGloss Estaz fuzzy garland fiber by Madeira as listed in color key
- #16 tapestry needle
- 7 (5mm) black round cabochons by The Beadery
- Fine iridescent glitter
- 6" square white felt
- White craft glue
- Hot-glue gun

Instructions

1. Cut plastic canvas according to graphs (also see page 134). Trim one outside row of holes from one heart shape for box bottom, which will remain unstitched. Using box bottom as a template, cut felt to use for lid lining.

2. Stitch pieces following graphs, reversing two arms and one nose before stitching. For bottom row of stitches on heart curves, stitch with white yarn first. Using 12" lengths, stitch fuzzy garland fiber over these white stitches, following Fig. 1, coming up at odd numbers and going down at even numbers.

3. Work pearl braid snowflakes over completed background stitching. Overcast head with white, heart with wine and pocket flaps with brisk green. Place pocket flaps on vest where indicated on graph; tack in place

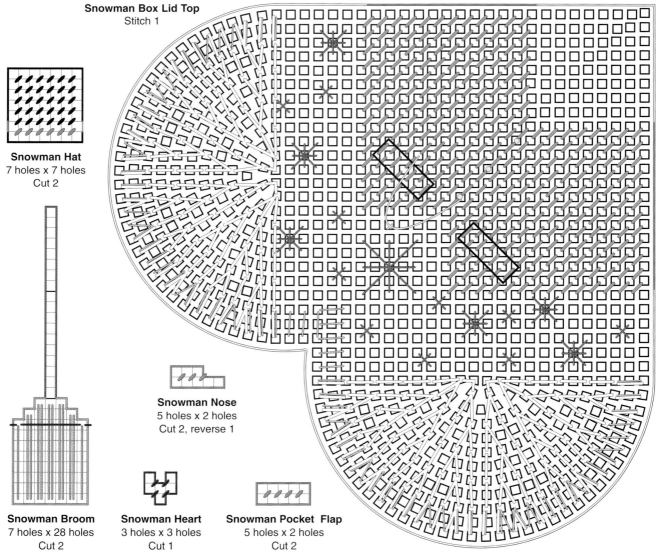

Snowman Box Lid Top
Stitch 1

Snowman Hat
7 holes x 7 holes
Cut 2

Snowman Nose
5 holes x 2 holes
Cut 2, reverse 1

Snowman Broom
7 holes x 28 holes
Cut 2

Snowman Heart
3 holes x 3 holes
Cut 1

Snowman Pocket Flap
5 holes x 2 holes
Cut 2

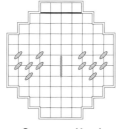

Snowman Head
10 holes x 11 holes
Cut 1

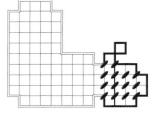

Snowman Arm
13 holes x 10 holes
Cut 4, reverse 2

COLOR KEY	
SNOWMAN SURPRISE BOX	
Plastic Canvas Yarn	**Yards**
☐ White #0001	55
▨ Pale pink #0003	½
■ Wine #0011	3
■ Brisk green #0027	7
■ Black #0028	2
▨ Orange #0030	1
Uncoded areas are white #0001 Continental Stitches	
✐ Walnut #0047 Overcasting	1
✐ Wine #0011 Backstitch	
✐ Almond #0057 Straight Stitch	2
Fuzzy Garland Fiber	
✐ Opalescent #01 over white #0001 yarn	3 cards
Medium (#16) Braid	
○ Aztec gold #202HL French Knot	1
ᴜ Aztec gold #202HL Couching Stitch	
Fine (#8) Braid	
✐ Pearl #032 Backstitch	2
ꜞ Attach nose	
☐ Pocket flap placement	
Color numbers given are for Spinrite plastic canvas yarn, WYndemasters GlissenGloss Estaz fuzzy garland fiber by Madeira and Kreinik Medium (#16) Braid and Fine (#8) Braid.	

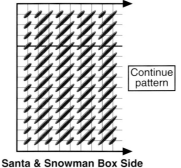

Santa & Snowman Box Side
62 holes x 14 holes
Cut 2 for Santa box,
stitch as graphed
Cut 2 for snowman box,
stitch with white

Continue pattern

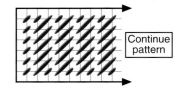

Continue pattern

Santa & Snowman Box Lid Side
66 holes x 7 holes
Cut 2 for Santa box lid,
stitch as graphed
Cut 2 for snowman box lid,
stitch with white

Snowman Hat Brim
12 holes x 6 holes
Cut 1

with brisk green. Following graph, couch a short length of gold braid for watch chain.

4. Whipstitch wrong sides of nose pieces together with orange; hot-glue to head where indicated on graph. Using photo as a guide, hot-glue two black cabochons to head for eyes and five cabochons under nose and cheeks for mouth.

5. With black, Overcast the bottom edges of the hat and the inside and outside edges of the hat brim. Whipstitch wrong sides of hat pieces together around side and top edges with brisk green and black. Using hot glue throughout, slip hat over head and glue in place. Slide brim over hat and glue in place. Glue heart to left side of hat front.

6. Using white throughout, with right sides together, Whipstitch short edges on one end of box sides together. Bring sides around and with wrong sides together, Whipstitch remaining short edges together, forming a heart. Aligning points, Whipstitch bottom edges of box

sides to box bottom, easing side pieces to fit around curves. Overcast top edges of box sides.

7. With right sides together, Whipstitch short edges on one end of lid sides together with white; bring sides around and with wrong sides together, Whipstitch remaining short edges together, forming a heart. Aligning points, and following lid top graph, Whipstitch top edges of lid sides to lid top, easing side pieces to fit around curve. Overcast bottom edges of lid sides with white. Glue white felt lining to wrong side of lid top.

8. With wrong sides together and matching edges, Whipstitch two arm pieces together with adjacent colors. Repeat with remaining two arm pieces. Whipstitch wrong sides of broom together following graph.

9. Using photo as guide, dip bottom end of broom in craft glue, then sprinkle with iridescent glitter. Shake off excess glitter; allow to dry. Hot-glue head to lid top at point, then glue broom and arms to vest.

Designed by Vicki Blizzard

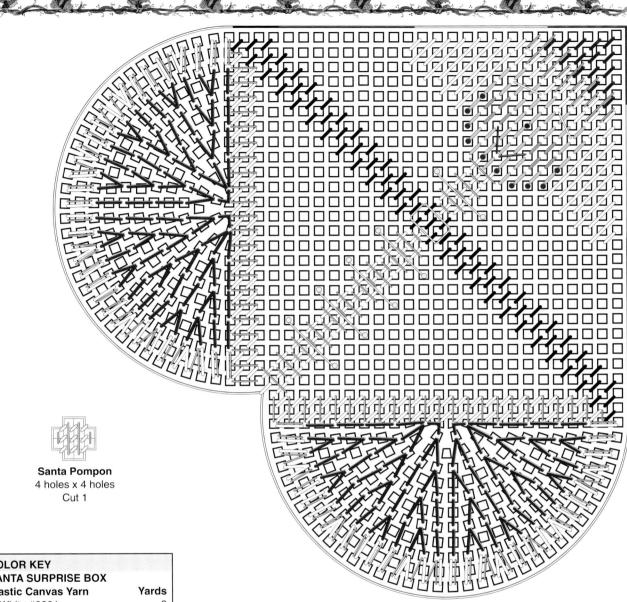

Santa Box Lid Top
Stitch 1

Santa Pompon
4 holes x 4 holes
Cut 1

COLOR KEY
SANTA SURPRISE BOX

Plastic Canvas Yarn	Yards
☐ White #0001	9
▦ Peach #0007	1
▦ Cherry pink #0010	½
■ Wine #0011	42
▦ Brisk green #0027	3
■ Black #0028	2

Uncoded areas are wine
#0011 Continental Stitches
⟋ White #0001 Straight Stitch
Scarlet #0022 Backstitch   ⅙

Fuzzy Garland Fiber
⟋ Opalescent #01 over   2 cards
white #0001 yarn

Medium (#16) Braid
⟋ Aztec gold #202HL Backstitch
and Straight Stitch   ½
● Attach beard
● Attach red bead
○ Attach gold bead

Color numbers given are for Spinrite plastic
canvas yarn, WYndemasters GlissenGloss
Estaz fuzzy garland fiber by Madeira and
Kreinik Medium (#16) Braid.

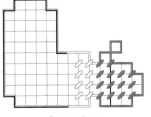

Santa Arm
13 holes x 10 holes
Cut 4, reverse 2

Comfort & Joy

Stitch a decorative reminder of the deeper meaning of Christmas with this inspirational wall hanging.

3. Using photo as a guide, glue ruffle to backside of stitched piece around edge. Cut beige ribbon in half. Glue one end of each half to backside where indicated on graph. Tie remaining ends together in a bow for hanging.

Designed by Michele Wilcox

Skill Level
Beginner

Materials
- 1 sheet 7-count plastic canvas
- Uniek Needloft plastic canvas yarn as listed in color key
- #3 pearl cotton as listed in color key
- 1 yard Christmas ruffle in coordinating colors (sample used 2¼"-wide ruffle)
- 1½ yards ⅜"-wide beige ribbon
- Hot-glue gun

Instructions
1. Cut plastic canvas according to graph.

2. Stitch piece following graph, working embroidery over completed background stitching. Overcast with crimson.

COLOR KEY	
Plastic Canvas Yarn	**Yards**
■ Black #00	8
▨ Cinnamon #14	3
▨ Holly #27	6
▨ Denim #33	8
■ Crimson #42	20
Uncoded areas are beige #40 Continental Stitches	30
● Holly #27 French Knot	
#3 Pearl Cotton	
╱ Black Backstitch	3
● Black French Knot	
○ Attach ribbon to backside	
Color numbers given are for Uniek Needloft plastic canvas yarn.	

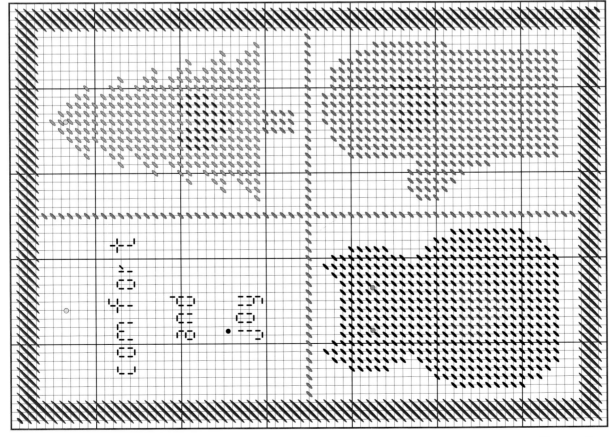

Comfort & Joy
50 holes x 70 holes
Cut 1

Christmas Cat

Cat lovers will adore a wall hanging of a cuddly black cat sitting on top of her Christmas gift. Hang it on a door or wall during the holidays.

Skill Level
Beginner

Materials
- 2 sheets 7-count plastic canvas
- Uniek Needloft plastic canvas yarn as listed in color key
- #3 pearl cotton as listed in color key
- 2 yards 1½"-wide gold wire-edged ribbon
- ½ yard ½"-wide red ribbon
- ½" jingle bell
- Hot-glue gun

Instructions

1. Cut plastic canvas according to graphs (also see page 140).

2. Stitch pieces following graphs, working gray pearl cotton Backstitches over completed background stitching. Overcast cat with black and package with holly.

3. Thread jingle bell on red ribbon and tie in a bow. Glue bow to cat where indicated on graph.

4. Using photo as a guide, wrap gold ribbon around package and tie in a bow. Glue bottom of cat to back top edge of package.

5. Hang as desired.

Designed by Michele Wilcox

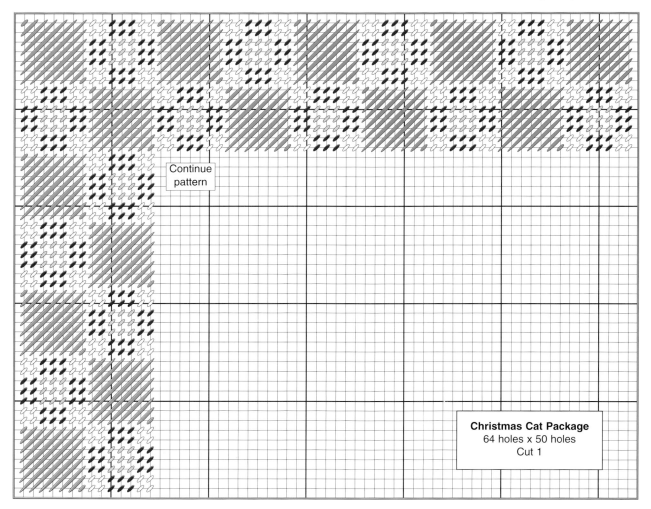

Continue pattern

Christmas Cat Package
64 holes x 50 holes
Cut 1

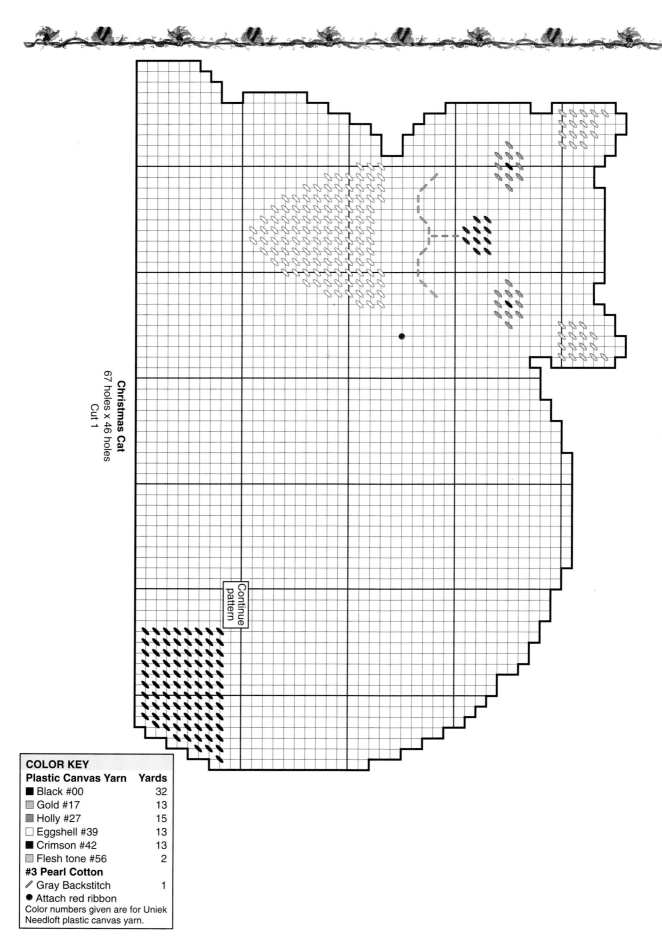

Christmas Cat
67 holes x 46 holes
Cut 1

Continue pattern

COLOR KEY

Plastic Canvas Yarn	Yards
■ Black #00	32
▨ Gold #17	13
▨ Holly #27	15
☐ Eggshell #39	13
■ Crimson #42	13
▨ Flesh tone #56	2
#3 Pearl Cotton	
✎ Gray Backstitch	1
● Attach red ribbon	

Color numbers given are for Uniek
Needloft plastic canvas yarn.

Fireplace Photo Frame

Capture your favorite Christmas memories in this charming photo frame! Mini stockings for each family member will delight one and all! See photo on page 143.

Skill Level
Beginner

Materials
- ½ sheet 7-count plastic canvas
- Spinrite Bernat Berella "4" worsted weight yarn as listed in color key
- Spinrite plastic canvas yarn as listed in color key
- Plastic Canvas 7 Metallic Needlepoint Yarn by Rainbow Gallery as listed in color key
- #16 tapestry needle
- Ceramic stocking buttons from Mill Hill Products by Gay Bowles Sales, Inc.:
  2 blue stockings #86111
  2 red stockings #86112
- Sewing needle and thread or floss to match buttons

Instructions

1. Cut plastic canvas according to graph (page 142).

2. Stitch piece following graph. Work medium taupe Backstitches and geranium French Knots with 2 plies yarn. Overcast edges following graph.

3. With sewing needle and matching thread or floss, attach buttons where indicated on graph. ***Note:** Buttons may be added or deleted, depending on family size.*

Designed by Joan Green

Christmas Notes

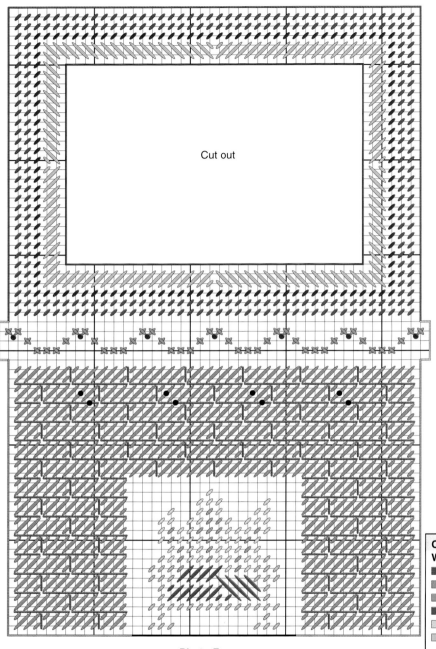

Photo Frame
45 holes x 66 holes
Cut 1

COLOR KEY

Worsted Weight Yarn	Yards
■ Medium taupe #8766	3
■ Honey #8795	14
□ Dark lagoon #8822	2
■ Medium navy #8838	8
□ Light tapestry gold #8886	1
□ Dark Oxford heather #8893	1
Uncoded areas on mantel are beige #8764 Continental Stitches	4
Uncoded areas in fire box are black #8994 Continental Stitches	3
╱ Medium taupe #8766 2-ply Backstitch	
● Geranium #8929 2-ply French Knot	½
Plastic Canvas Yarn	
□ Orange #0030	1
⅛"Metallic Needlepoint Yarn	
□ Gold #PC 1	4
■ Dark gold #PC 18	5
● Attach buttons	

Color numbers given are for Spinrite Bernat Berella "4" worsted weight yarn, Spinrite plastic canvas yarn and Rainbow Gallery Plastic Canvas 7 Metallic Needlepoint Yarn.

Let It Snow!

Christmas Countdown Tree

Instructions begin on page 150

Snowman Carolers

Join this family of snow people as they sing your favorite Christmas carols! They'll add a lot to the holiday spirit in your home.

Skill Level
Advanced beginner

Materials
- 2 sheets 7-count Ultra Stiff plastic canvas by Darice
- Spinrite plastic canvas yarn as listed in color key
- DMC 6-strand embroidery floss as listed in color key
- 6" ¼"-wide red satin ribbon
- 5mm white pompon
- 2 small gilded birch pinecones
- Assorted artificial or dried red and white berries
- Scraps artificial evergreen
- Small amount white floral wire
- Low-temperature glue gun

Cutting & Stitching

1. Cut plastic canvas according to graphs (pages 147 through 149).

2. Stitch pieces following graphs, reversing one background before stitching. Stitch two large arms as graphed, reversing one before stitching. Repeat with remaining two large arms, replacing wine with clover.

3. Stitch two small arms as graphed, reversing one before stitching. Repeat with remaining two small arms, replacing wine with brisk green.

4. Stitch one large and one small songbook as graphed. Stitch remaining songbooks with brisk green. Work embroidery on lamppost, faces and background.

5. Overcast lamppost with black. Following graphs and

using adjacent colors throughout, Whipstitch center seam of background pieces together. Overcast all other background edges. Overcast all remaining pieces. Backstitch spines on songbooks.

Assembly

1. Using photo as a guide throughout assembly and making sure bottom edges are even, glue lamppost to center seam and one small body on each side of lamppost. Glue one large body on the left side of small bodies and one large body on the right of small bodies.

2. Glue large green songbook and large arms with wine mittens to large body on the left, then glue on father's head and hat. Glue large wine songbook and large arms with clover mittens to large body on the right, then glue on mother's head and hat.

3. Glue small green songbook and small arms with wine mittens to small body on the left, then glue on girl's head and hat. Glue small wine songbook and small arms with brisk green mittens to small body on the right, then glue on boy's head. Glue earmuffs to

boy's head, placing ends of floral wire between head and earmuffs before gluing in place.

4. Glue pompon to tip of girl's hat. Glue small sprig of evergreen and one pinecone to right side of father's hat. Glue a bit of evergreen and remaining pinecone under lamp on lamppost. Glue berries to mother's hat.

5. Tie ribbon in a bow and glue under pinecone on lamppost. Trim tails as desired.

6. Place finished piece over doorway; fasten as desired.

Designed by Celia Lange Designs

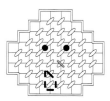

Girl's Head
9 holes x 8 holes
Cut 1

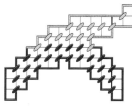

Girl's Hat
12 holes x 9 holes
Cut 1

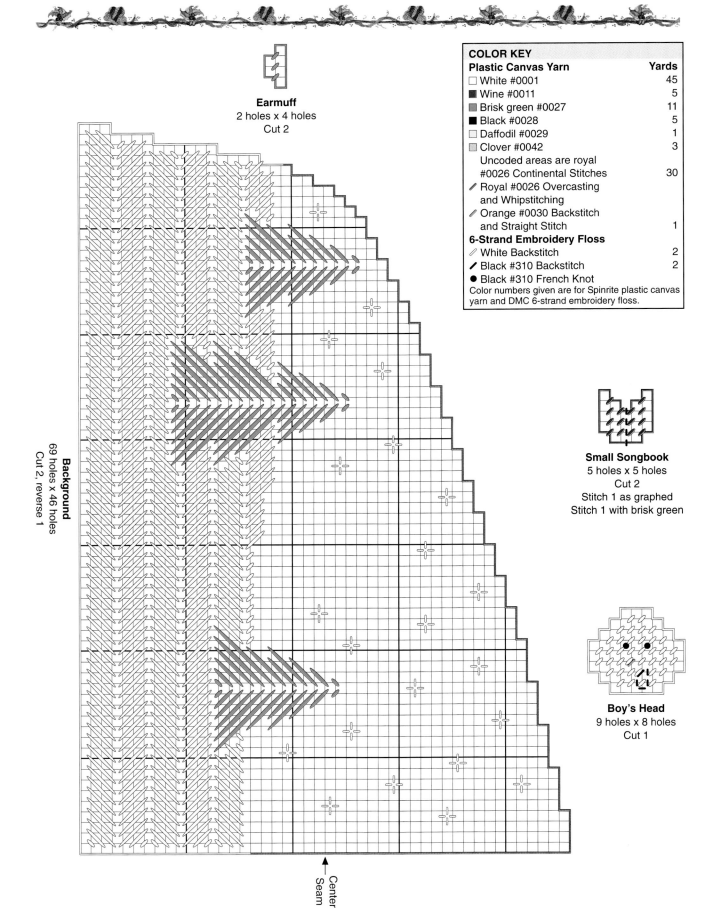

Earmuff
2 holes x 4 holes
Cut 2

Background
69 holes x 46 holes
Cut 2, reverse 1

COLOR KEY

Plastic Canvas Yarn	Yards
□ White #0001	45
■ Wine #0011	5
▨ Brisk green #0027	11
■ Black #0028	5
□ Daffodil #0029	1
▨ Clover #0042	3
Uncoded areas are royal #0026 Continental Stitches	30
╱ Royal #0026 Overcasting and Whipstitching	
╱ Orange #0030 Backstitch and Straight Stitch	1
6-Strand Embroidery Floss	
╱ White Backstitch	2
╱ Black #310 Backstitch	2
● Black #310 French Knot	

Color numbers given are for Spinrite plastic canvas yarn and DMC 6-strand embroidery floss.

Small Songbook
5 holes x 5 holes
Cut 2
Stitch 1 as graphed
Stitch 1 with brisk green

Boy's Head
9 holes x 8 holes
Cut 1

Center
Seam

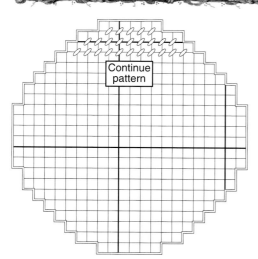

Large Body
22 holes x 22 holes
Cut 2

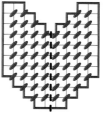

Large Songbook
9 holes x 10 holes
Cut 2
Stitch 1 as graphed
Stitch 1 with brisk green

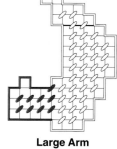

Large Arm
10 holes x 13 holes
Cut 2, reverse 1,
stitch as graphed
Cut 2, reverse 1,
replacing wine with clover

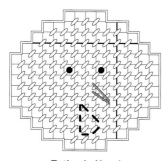

Small Arm
6 holes x 8 holes
Cut 2, reverse 1,
stitch as graphed
Cut 2, reverse 1,
replacing wine with brisk green

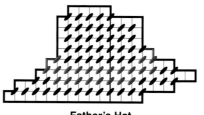

Small Body
13 holes x 13 holes
Cut 2

Father's Head
14 holes x 13 holes
Cut 1

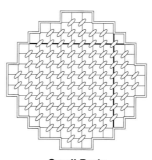

Father's Hat
18 holes x 9 holes
Cut 1

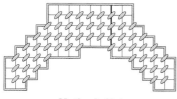

Mother's Hat
16 holes x 8 holes
Cut 1

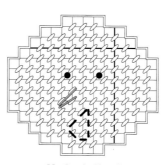

Mother's Head
14 holes x 13 holes
Cut 1

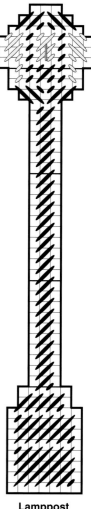

Lamppost
9 holes x 46 holes
Cut 1

Christmas Countdown Tree

The days before Christmas are filled with such wonderful expectation! Heighten your children's excitement by counting down the days with this colorful tree. See the photo on page 144.

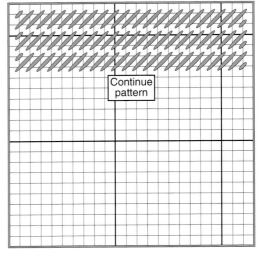

Skill Level
Beginner

Materials
- 2 sheets 7-count Ultra Stiff plastic canvas by Darice
- Spinrite plastic canvas yarn as listed in color key
- DMC 6-strand embroidery floss as listed in color key
- 24 small pieces or dots hook-side Velcro hook-and-loop tape
- Low-temperature glue gun

Instructions

1. Cut plastic canvas according to graphs (also see pages 152 and 153).

2. Stitch base pieces, tree skirt, tree, star and packages following graphs, reversing one base side before stitching. Backstitch numbers on packages and star when background stitching is completed, then Overcast with adjacent colors.

3. Cut a short length of yarn to match the ribbon on each package. Thread the yarn from back to front where indicated on the graph, tie in a bow and trim ends as desired.

4. Overcast tree skirt with crimson and white following graph. Using brisk green throughout, Overcast tree. Whipstitch base front to base sides following graphs. Whipstitch base sides to base back, then Whipstitch front, back and sides to base bottom.

5. Glue tree skirt to base front, making sure bottom edges are even. Glue tree to base front, placing bottom edge of tree directly above top edge of tree skirt.

6. Continental Stitch background on ornaments with colors indicated on Ornament Chart. Overcast with adjacent colors. Following Ornament Chart and numbers graph, center and embroider numbers on each ornament. Glue hook-and-loop tape dots to back of star and each ornament and package.

7. Store ornaments, packages and star in base box

behind tree. Beginning on Dec. 1 each year, attach each day's ornament to tree or package under tree. On Christmas Eve, place star at top of tree.

Designed by Celia Lange Designs

Base Bottom
23 holes x 23 holes
Cut 1

COLOR KEY

Plastic Canvas Yarn	Yards
☐ White #0001	3
◼ Royal #0026	9
▨ Brisk green #0027	52
◼ Crimson #0032	11
☐ Mustard #0043	11
⁄ Brisk green #0027 Backstitch	
6-Strand Embroidery Floss	
⁄ White Backstitch	2
⁄ Christmas red #321 Backstitch	½
⁄ Christmas green #909 Backstitch	2
⁄ Christmas gold #972 Backstitch	2
● Attach bow	

Color numbers given are for Spinrite plastic canvas yarn and DMC 6-strand embroidery floss.

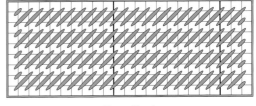

Base Back
23 holes x 9 holes
Cut 1

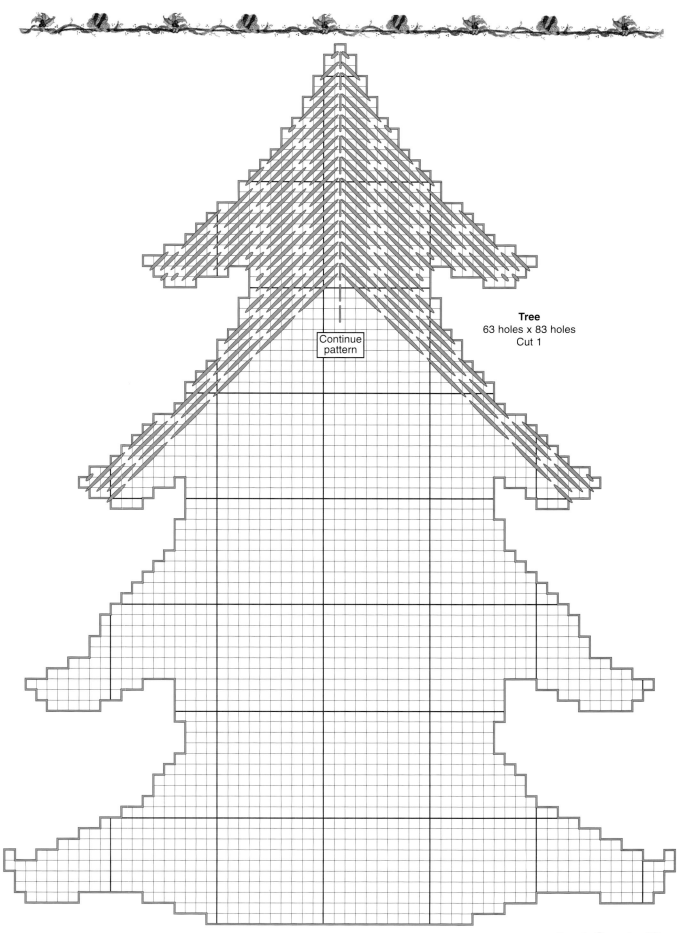

Tree
63 holes x 83 holes
Cut 1

Continue
pattern

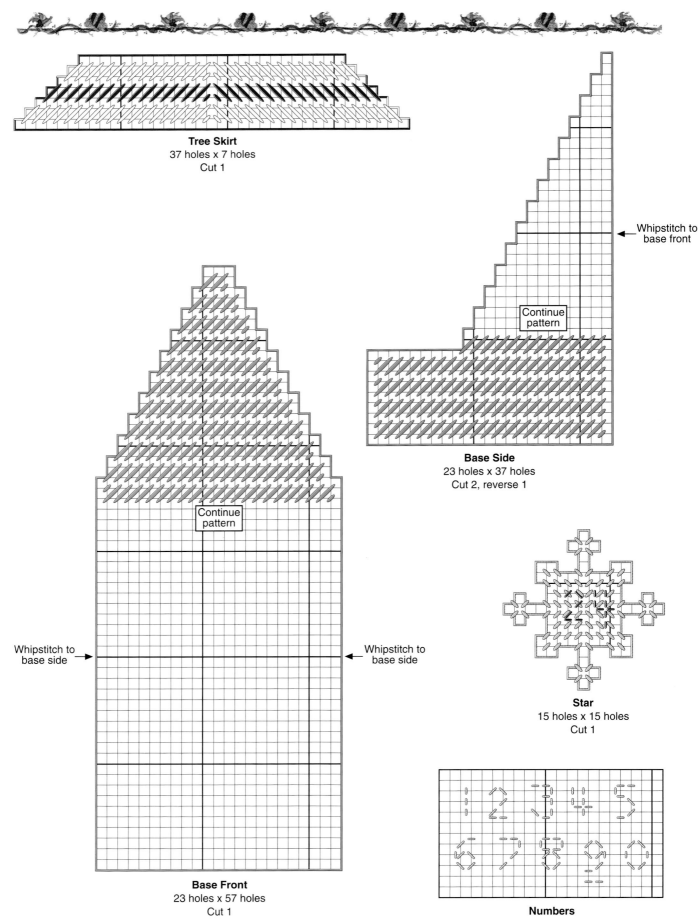

Tree Skirt
37 holes x 7 holes
Cut 1

Whipstitch to
base front

Continue
pattern

Base Side
23 holes x 37 holes
Cut 2, reverse 1

Continue
pattern

Whipstitch to
base side

Whipstitch to
base side

Star
15 holes x 15 holes
Cut 1

Base Front
23 holes x 57 holes
Cut 1

Numbers

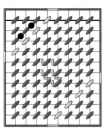

Package 1
9 holes x 11 holes
Cut 1

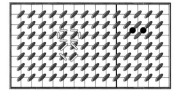

Package 2
15 holes x 8 holes
Cut 1

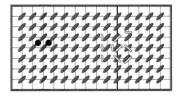

Package 4
15 holes x 8 holes
Cut 1

COLOR KEY

Plastic Canvas Yarn	Yards
☐ White #0001	3
■ Royal #0026	9
■ Brisk green #0027	52
■ Crimson #0032	11
☐ Mustard #0043	11
⁄ Brisk green #0027 Backstitch	

6-Strand Embroidery Floss

⁄ White Backstitch	2
⁄ Christmas red #321 Backstitch	½
⁄ Christmas green #909 Backstitch	2
⁄ Christmas gold #972 Backstitch	2
● Attach bow	

Color numbers given are for Spinrite plastic canvas yarn and DMC 6-strand embroidery floss.

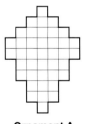

Package 3
11 holes x 9 holes
Cut 1

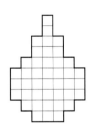

Package 5
11 holes x 11 holes
Cut 1

ORNAMENT CHART

Date	Ornament	Background Yarn Color	Embroidery Floss Color
1	A	Royal	Christmas gold
2	C	Crimson	White
3	B	Mustard	Christmas green
5	A	Crimson	White
6	C	Mustard	Christmas green
7	B	Royal	Christmas gold
9	A	Mustard	Christmas green
10	C	Royal	Christmas gold
11	B	Crimson	White
13	A	Royal	Christmas gold
14	C	Crimson	White
15	B	Mustard	Christmas green
17	A	Crimson	White
18	C	Mustard	Christmas green
19	B	Royal	Christmas gold
21	A	Mustard	Christmas green
22	C	Royal	Christmas gold
23	B	Crimson	White

Ornament A
7 holes x 10 holes
Cut 6
Continental Stitch and Backstitch
following Ornament Chart
and instructions

Ornament B
7 holes x 10 holes
Cut 6
Continental Stitch and Backstitch
following Ornament Chart
and instructions

Ornament C
6 holes x 8 holes
Cut 6
Continental Stitch and Backstitch
following Ornament Chart
and instructions

Christmas Remembered

Keep those Christmases captured on video close at hand by storing the tape in a decorative holder you'll recognize at a glance!

Skill Level
Intermediate

Materials
- 2 sheets 7-count plastic canvas
- Spinrite plastic canvas yarn as listed in color key
- DMC #3 pearl cotton as listed in color key
- Gold Rush ¹⁄₁₆"-wide metallic ribbon by Rainbow Gallery as listed in color key
- 1 sheet tan felt
- Thick tacky craft glue

Instructions
1. Cut plastic canvas according to graphs.

2. Work background with almond and natural Alternating Continental Stitches and brisk green Cross Stitches following graphs. Work embroidery over completed background stitching. Do not stitch medium garnet lettering on bottom.

3. Using all pieces as templates, cut felt lining slightly smaller than pieces. Glue linings to wrong sides of pieces. Allow to dry.

4. Using almond throughout, Overcast the bottom edges of the top, bottom and side pieces from dot to dot. Whipstitch the top, bottom and sides together, then Whipstitch back piece to unstitched edges of top, bottom and sides.

Designed by Celia Lange Designs

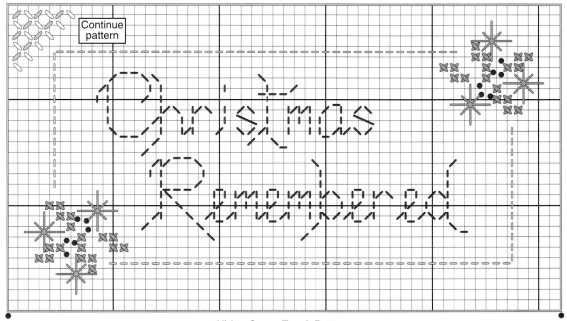

Video Cover Top & Bottom
52 holes x 29 holes
Cut 2
Omit lettering on bottom

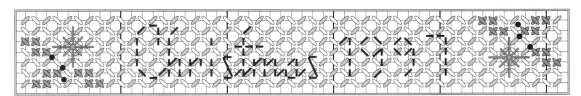

Video Cover Back
52 holes x 8 holes
Cut 1

COLOR KEY

Plastic Canvas Yarn		Yards
☐ Natural #0002		21
◼ Brisk green #0027		5
◻ Almond #0056		27
#3 Pearl Cotton		
✎ Medium garnet #815 Backstitch		10
● Medium garnet #815 French Knot		
¹⁄₁₆ " Metallic Ribbon		
✎ Gold #X2 Backstitch		4
✎ Silver #X5 Straight Stitch		5

Color numbers given are for Spinrite plastic canvas yarn, DMC #3 pearl cotton and Rainbow Gallery Gold Rush metallic ribbon.

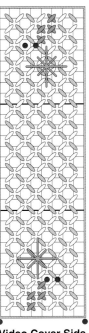

Video Cover Side
8 holes x 29 holes
Cut 2

Christmas Journal

Jot down your favorite Christmas memories in a special holiday journal. You'll love reliving all those unforgettable moments for many years to come.

Skill Level
Beginner

Materials
- 1 sheet 7-count plastic canvas
- Uniek Needloft plastic canvas yarn as listed in color key
- DMC #3 pearl cotton as listed in color key
- 1 yard 1⅜"-wide gold wire-edged ribbon
- 2 (1¼") book rings
- 3¾" x 6¾" loose-leaf notebook paper

Instructions

1. Cut plastic canvas according to graph.

2. Continental Stitch cover pieces with eggshell, crimson and holly following graph. When Continental Stitching is completed, work medium emerald green Backstitches and bright Christmas red French Knots.

3. Overcast inner book ring edges with eggshell and all remaining edges with crimson.

4. Place notebook paper between covers; insert book rings through holes. Wrap ribbon around journal and tie in a bow; trim edges as desired.

Designed by Michele Wilcox

COLOR KEY	
Plastic Canvas Yarn	**Yards**
▨ Holly #27	12
▪ Crimson #42	15
Uncoded areas are eggshell #39 Continental Stitches	30
⁄ Eggshell #39 Overcasting	
#3 Pearl Cotton	**Skeins**
● Bright Christmas red #666 French Knot	1
⁄ Medium emerald green #911 Backstitch	1
Color numbers given are for Uniek Needloft plastic canvas yarn and DMC #3 pearl cotton.	

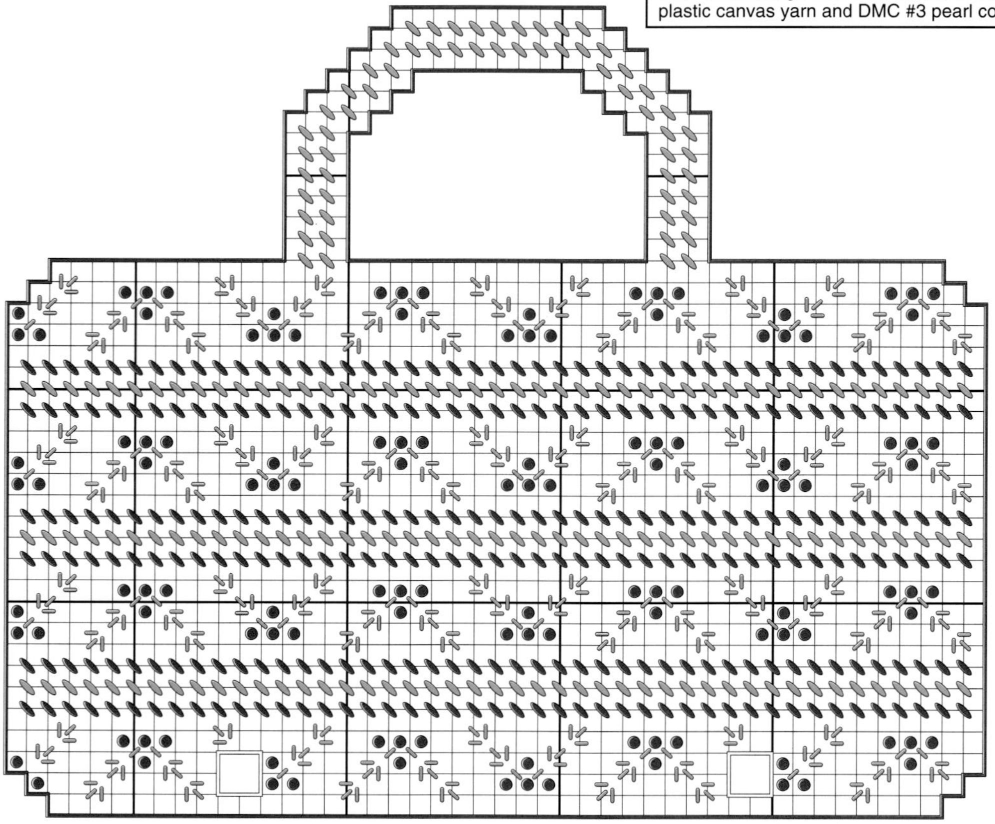

Journal Cover
38 holes x 46 holes
Cut 2

We Believe in Santa

Children will especially love this wintry wall hanging as they look forward to Santa's visit on Christmas Eve!

Skill Level
Beginner

Materials
- 1 sheet 7-count plastic canvas
- Spinrite Bernat Berella "4" worsted weight yarn as listed in color key
- #16 tapestry needle
- Ceramic buttons from Mill Hill Products by Gay Bowles Sales, Inc.:
  Santa Face #86008
  Gold Star #86016
  Crescent Santa #86153
  Candy Cane Santa #86154
  Star Santa #86155
- Sewing needle and thread or floss to match buttons
- Sawtooth hanger
- Hot-glue gun (optional)

Instructions

1. Cut plastic canvas according to graph.

2. Stitch piece following graph. When background stitching is completed, Backstitch remainder of letters with 4 plies white. Work Backstitches on Santa with 2 plies dark Oxford heather.

3. Overcast corners with dark lagoon and remainder of edges with geranium.

4. With sewing needle and matching thread or floss, attach gold star button at tip of Santa's hat where indicated on graph. Sew Santa buttons in four corners.

5. Glue or sew sawtooth hanger to center top on backside of finished piece.

Designed by Joan Green

COLOR KEY	
Worsted Weight Yarn	**Yards**
■ Dark lagoon #8822	6
■ Geranium #8929	14
□ Winter white #8941	20
□ Light peach #8977	½
■ Black #8994	¼
Uncoded areas are navy #8965 Continental Stitches	38
✎ Dark Oxford heather #8893 2-ply Backstitch	½
✎ Winter white #8941 4-ply Backstitch	
○ Attach star button	
Color numbers given are for Spinrite Bernat Berella "4" worsted weight yarn.	

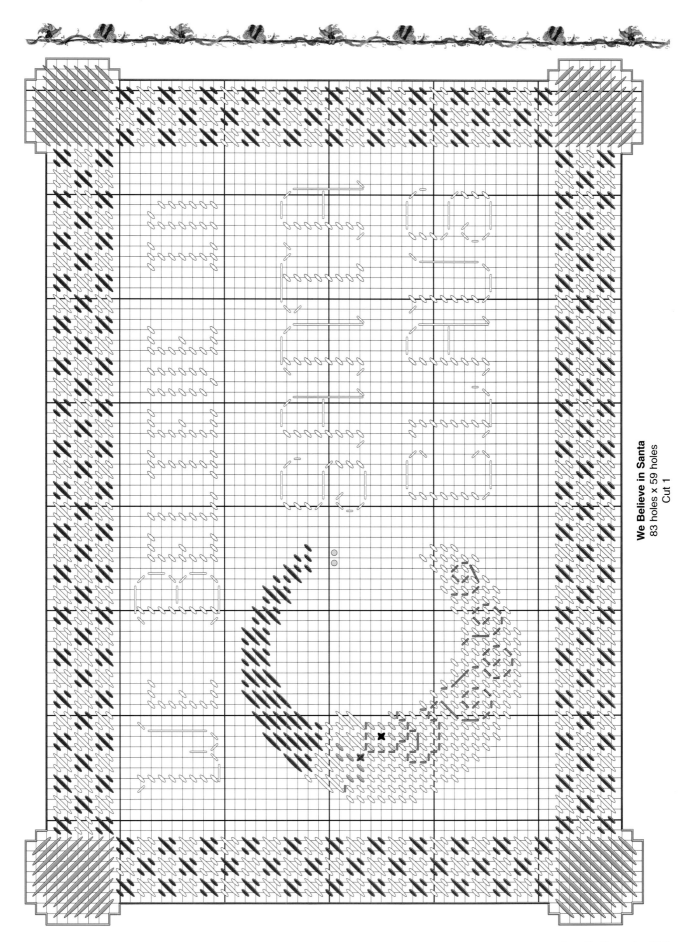

We Believe in Santa
83 holes x 59 holes
Cut 1

Country Snowmen

Give your home a tea-dyed look with this set of decorative snowmen! A basket add-on, doorknob hanger and attractive sign will add a pleasant country touch to your decor!

Basket Add-On

Skill Level
Beginner

Materials
- ⅓ sheet 7-count plastic canvas
- Uniek Needloft plastic canvas yarn as listed in color key
- Small amount beige #3 pearl cotton and as listed in color key
- 4 buttons in various sizes and colors
- 8" ¾"-wide checkered craft ribbon (sample used navy and beige)
- 10" strip 1"-wide flowered flannel (sample used dark green with garnet and beige flowers)
- Small silk sunflower
- 2 (3"-long) twigs
- Small basket with handle
- Hot-glue gun

Instructions
1. Cut plastic canvas according to graph.

2. Continental Stitch piece following graph. Work embroidery when Continental Stitching is completed. Overcast with black and beige following graph.

3. Using photo as guide through step 4, sew buttons to snowman body with beige pearl cotton. Fold checkered ribbon in half lengthwise and tie around hat. Trim ends as desired. Glue sunflower over ribbon knot.

4. Fold flannel in half lengthwise and tie around neck; trim ends as desired. Glue twigs to backside of snowman for arms. Glue snowman to basket.

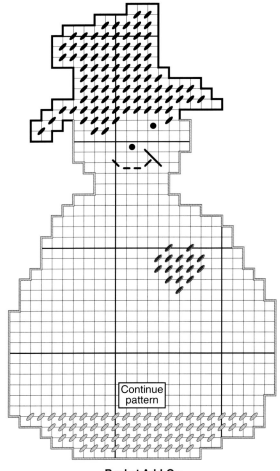

Basket Add-On
25 holes x 43 holes
Cut 1

```
Continue
pattern
```

COLOR KEY	
BASKET ADD-ON	
Plastic Canvas Yarn	**Yards**
■ Black #00	2
▨ Beige #40	12
■ Crimson #42	1
#3 Pearl Cotton	
✎ Black Backstitch	½
● Black French Knot	
Color numbers given are for Uniek Needloft plastic canvas yarn.	

Doorknob Hanger

Materials
- ½ sheet 7-count plastic canvas
- Uniek Needloft plastic canvas yarn as listed in color key
- Small amount beige #3 pearl cotton and as listed in color key
- 5 buttons in various sizes and colors
- 1 yard thin wire
- 10" ¾"-wide checkered craft ribbon (sample used navy and beige)

Materials listing continued on page 162

- 16" strip 1½"-wide flowered flannel (sample used dark green with garnet and beige flowers)
- Small silk sunflower
- 2 (4"-long) twigs
- Hot-glue gun

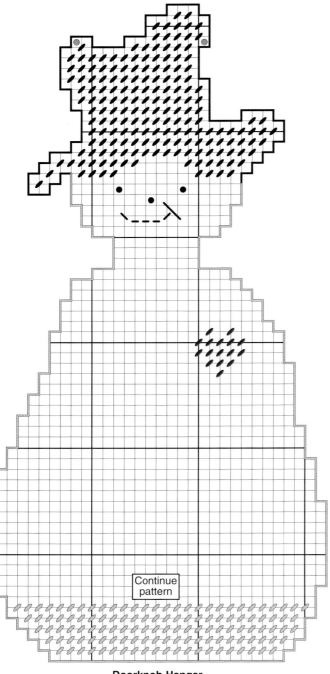

Doorknob Hanger
32 holes x 62 holes
Cut 1

Instructions

1. Cut plastic canvas according to graph.

2. Continental Stitch piece following graph. Work embroidery when Continental Stitching is completed. Overcast with black and beige following graph.

3. Cut wire in half and place lengths together, matching ends. Using photo as a guide through step 5, thread double ends through hole indicated with blue dot on left side of hat, then thread remaining ends through hole indicated with blue dot on right side of hat. Pull approximately 3" through on both sides and wrap ends around wire to secure. Wrap ends around pencil to make tendrils.

4. Sew buttons to snowman body with beige pearl cotton. Fold checkered ribbon in half lengthwise and tie around hat. Trim ends as desired. Glue sunflower over ribbon knot.

5. Fold flannel in half lengthwise and tie around neck; trim ends as desired. Glue twigs to backside of snowman for arms.

Sign

Materials

- 1 sheet 7-count plastic canvas
- Uniek Needloft plastic canvas yarn as listed in color key
- 1 yard beige #3 pearl cotton and as listed in color key
- 2 (⅜") black buttons
- 5 buttons in various sizes and colors
- ½ yard ¼"-wide off-white ribbon
- 12" 1½"-wide checkered craft ribbon (sample used navy and beige)
- 18" strip 2½"-wide flowered flannel (sample used dark green with garnet and beige flowers)
- Small silk sunflower with leaves
- 2 (5"-long) small branches
- Hot-glue gun

Instructions

1. Cut plastic canvas according to graphs (also see page 164).

2. Stitch pieces following graphs. Work embroidery

COLOR KEY	
DOORKNOB HANGER	
Plastic Canvas Yarn	**Yards**
■ Black #00	4
▨ Beige #40	22
■ Crimson #42	1
#3 Pearl Cotton	
╱ Black Backstitch	½
● Black French Knot	
Color numbers given are for Uniek Needloft plastic canvas yarn.	

when background stitching is completed. Overcast sign with beige and snowman with black and beige following graphs.

3. Using beige pearl cotton, sew ⅜" buttons to head where indicated on graph with blue dots; sew five remaining buttons to snowman body. Fold checkered ribbon in half lengthwise and tie around hat. Trim ends as desired. Glue sunflower and leaves over ribbon knot.

4. Fold flannel in half lengthwise and tie around neck; trim ends as desired. Glue one branch to backside of snowman and one to front of snowman for arms.

5. Cut off-white ribbon in half; thread through cutouts at top of sign and through holes indicated at bottom of snowman graph. Adjust ribbon so sign hangs freely, then tie each in a bow. Trim ends as desired.

6. Hang as desired.

Designed by Michele Wilcox

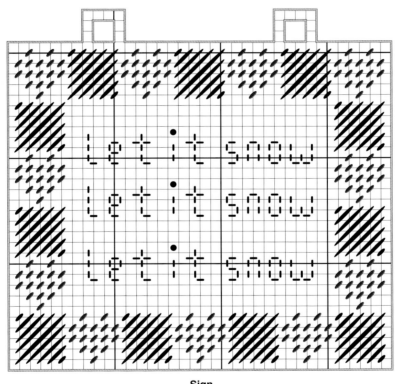

Sign
36 holes x 34 holes
Cut 1

COLOR KEY
SIGN

Plastic Canvas Yarn	Yards
■ Black #00	15
☐ Beige #40	55
■ Crimson #42	5
Uncoded areas on sign are beige #40 Continental Stitches	

#3 Pearl Cotton

╱ Black Backstitch	3
● Black French Knot	
● Attach ribbon	

Color numbers given are for Uniek Needloft plastic canvas yarn.

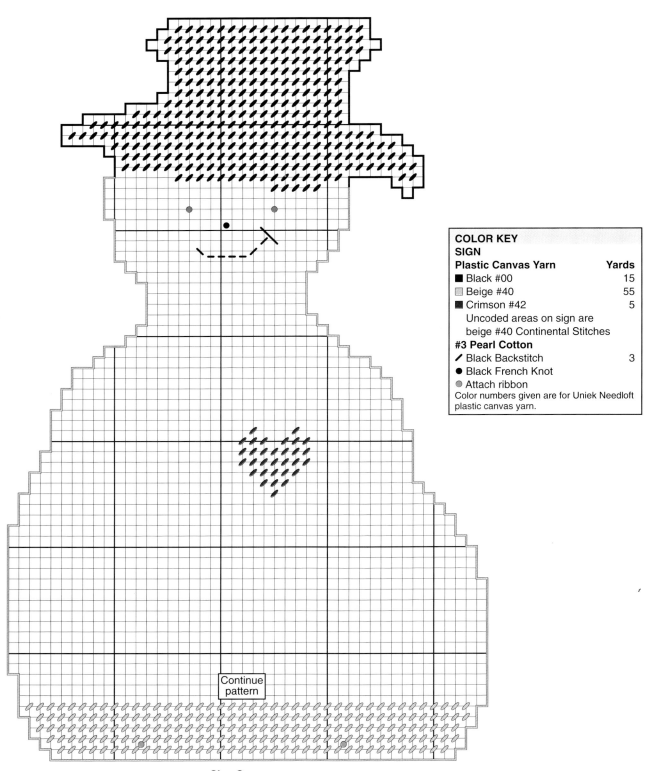

COLOR KEY
SIGN

Plastic Canvas Yarn	Yards
■ Black #00	15
■ Beige #40	55
■ Crimson #42	5

Uncoded areas on sign are
beige #40 Continental Stitches

#3 Pearl Cotton

✁ Black Backstitch	3
● Black French Knot	
● Attach ribbon	

Color numbers given are for Uniek Needloft
plastic canvas yarn.

Continue
pattern

Sign Snowman
45 holes x 70 holes
Cut 1

Snow-Lady Angel

If you include angels in your holiday decorating, you'll surely want to include this little beauty! With her long eyelashes, plump body and white curly hair, she'll win your heart!

Skill Level

Intermediate

Materials

- 1 sheet 7-count plastic canvas
- 2 (5") plastic canvas star shapes by Uniek
- 2 (6") plastic canvas heart shapes by Uniek
- 4" plastic canvas radial circle by Uniek
- Spinrite plastic canvas yarn as listed in color key
- Kreinik ⅛" Ribbon as listed in color key
- DMC #3 pearl cotton as listed in color key
- Glass seed beads by Mill Hill Products from Gay Bowles Sales, Inc., as listed in color key
- #16 tapestry needle
- 2 (15mm) black round cabochons by The Beadery
- 5 (8mm) black round cabochons by The Beadery
- White Maxi-Curl doll hair by One & Only Creations
- 1 yard ¼"-wide rose satin ribbon
- 1 yard ¼"-wide jade satin ribbon
- ½ yard 2"-wide white iridescent lace
- ½ yard white broadcloth
- Sewing needle and white sewing thread
- 3" wooden craft stick or round toothpick
- Polyester fiberfill
- Polyester stuffing pellets or rice in plastic bag (optional, for weight)
- Hot-glue gun

Cutting & Stitching

1. Cut plastic canvas according to graphs (pages 167 and 170). Carefully cut purchased 6" heart shapes in half down center in order to use both halves from each shape. Cut seven outside rows from each star shape.

2. Stitch pieces following graphs, reversing one nose and one hand before stitching. Stitch one heart appliqué as graphed and one replacing geranium with sage and pale pink with seafoam.

3. Work black pearl cotton Backstitches on head front only. Work beading (see step 4) on one star wand piece when background stitching is completed.

4. For beading, use sewing needle and white thread. Bring needle up in bottom hole of one star section, thread one aquamarine bead then six pink beads; bring needle down through same hole. Secure top of loop as in a Lazy Daisy Stitch where indicated on beading graph, making sure there are three pink beads on each side of securing stitch. Work beading in remaining four sections.

5. Using white throughout, for head front and with right sides together, Whipstitch dart at top together, then Whipstitch dart at head bottom together. Repeat with head back. With wrong sides together, Whipstitch head front and back together around sides and top from dot to dot. Stuff head firmly with fiberfill, then Whipstitch bottom edges together.

6. Whipstitch wrong sides of nose together with light orange, stuffing lightly with fiberfill before closing. Overcast cheeks, hands, holly leaves and heart berries with adjacent colors. Overcast heart appliqués with the darker of the two colors.

7. Using geranium throughout, with wrong sides together and matching edges, Whipstitch two wing pieces together around curved edges, forming one wing. Repeat with remaining two wing pieces, forming second wing. Whipstitch two wings together along cut center edges.

8. Whipstitch wrong sides of star shapes together with pearl ribbon, working two stitches per hole as necessary to cover plastic canvas. Insert wooden craft stick or toothpick into star for handle.

9. Cut one 16" circle for body and two 4" circles for sleeves from broadcloth. Fold raw edges of circles under ⅛" and press in place.

Assembly

1. Using photo as a guide throughout assembly, glue nose to center of face where indicated on graph. Glue large cabochons to face for eyes. Glue cheeks in place, then glue small cabochons to face for mouth.

2. Glue hair to head as desired, following manufacturer's directions. For halo, glue tops and bottoms of leaves together, forming a circle. Glue one heart berry

to top of each leaf, leaving two adjacent leaves without heart berries. Making sure leaves without heart berries are at the bottom, glue halo to top of head, pressing firmly to secure glue through hair.

3. With sewing needle and thread, stitch a running stitch around outside edge of body circle; pull thread to gather. While gathering, insert 4" plastic canvas circle in bottom center, then optional bag with stuffing pellets or rice. Complete stuffing lightly with fiberfill, leaving a 1" opening. Secure thread by knotting several times.

4. Make a hole in center of body stuffing. Insert neck part of head into hole and glue in place. With sewing needle and thread, make a running stitch along straight edge of lace, pulling tightly. Secure with a knot. Glue lace around neck edge.

5. Repeat step 3 with sleeves, stuffing only with fiberfill and leaving a ¾" opening. Insert hands into openings

and glue or tack in place with sewing thread. Glue wooden craft stick or toothpick on wand to backside of angel's left hand. Glue arms and hands to body, then glue heart appliqués to body front.

6. Cut one 8" length, one 10" length and one 18" length from each color of ¼"-wide ribbon. Tie a small bow with 8" and 10" lengths. Trim tails of 8" bows, then glue jade bow to bottom of geranium heart and rose bow to bottom of sage heart.

7. Glue jade bow with long tails to bottom of star on wand. Glue rose bow directly on top of jade bow. Trim ends as desired.

8. Tie medium bows with remaining 18" lengths of ribbon. Glue rose bow to halo over leaves with no heart berries. Glue jade ribbon directly over rose bow. Trim ends as desired.

Designed by Vicki Blizzard

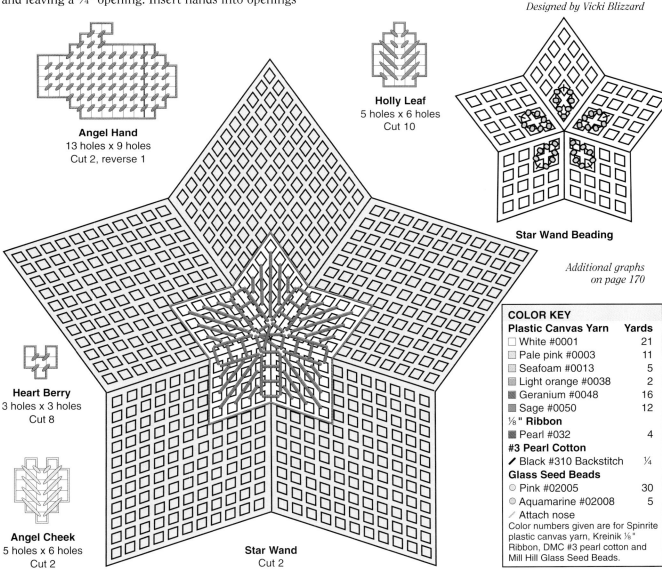

Angel Hand
13 holes x 9 holes
Cut 2, reverse 1

Holly Leaf
5 holes x 6 holes
Cut 10

Star Wand Beading

Additional graphs on page 170

Heart Berry
3 holes x 3 holes
Cut 8

Angel Cheek
5 holes x 6 holes
Cut 2

Star Wand
Cut 2

COLOR KEY

Plastic Canvas Yarn	Yards
☐ White #0001	21
☐ Pale pink #0003	11
☐ Seafoam #0013	5
☐ Light orange #0038	2
☐ Geranium #0048	16
☐ Sage #0050	12
⅛" Ribbon	
☐ Pearl #032	4
#3 Pearl Cotton	
✎ Black #310 Backstitch	¼
Glass Seed Beads	
○ Pink #02005	30
○ Aquamarine #02008	5
✎ Attach nose	

Color numbers given are for Spinrite plastic canvas yarn, Kreinik ⅛" Ribbon, DMC #3 pearl cotton and Mill Hill Glass Seed Beads.

Merry Little Christmas

Everyone wishes for a white Christmas, and with this charming sign, whether it snows or not, you'll always have one!

Experience Level
Beginner

Materials
- 1 sheet 7-count plastic canvas
- Uniek Needloft plastic canvas yarn as listed in color key
- DMC #3 pearl cotton as listed in color key
- 2 yards 1¼"-wide gold wire-edged ribbon
- 2 small bunches artificial holly
- 2 small bunches artificial pine
- Hot-glue gun

Instructions

1. Cut plastic canvas according to graph.

2. Continental Stitch piece following graph. Work embroidery when Continental Stitching is completed. Overcast piece with Christmas green.

3. Using photo as a guide throughout, glue pine at top of stitched piece. Glue holly in center of pine. Tie ribbon in a bow, trimming ends as desired. Glue bow above holly.

4. Hang as desired.

Designed by Michele Wilcox

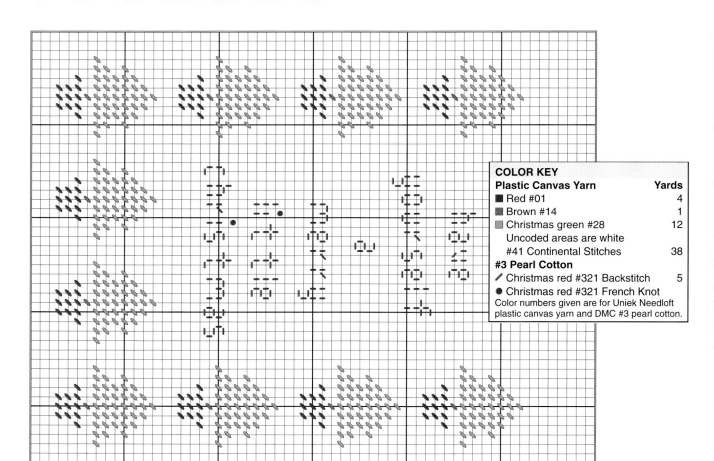

COLOR KEY

Plastic Canvas Yarn	Yards
■ Red #01	4
▨ Brown #14	1
▦ Christmas green #28	12
Uncoded areas are white #41 Continental Stitches	38
#3 Pearl Cotton	
╱ Christmas red #321 Backstitch	5
● Christmas red #321 French Knot	

Color numbers given are for Uniek Needloft plastic canvas yarn and DMC #3 pearl cotton.

Merry Little Christmas Sign
47 holes x 60 holes
Cut 1

Snow-Lady Angel

Continued from page 167

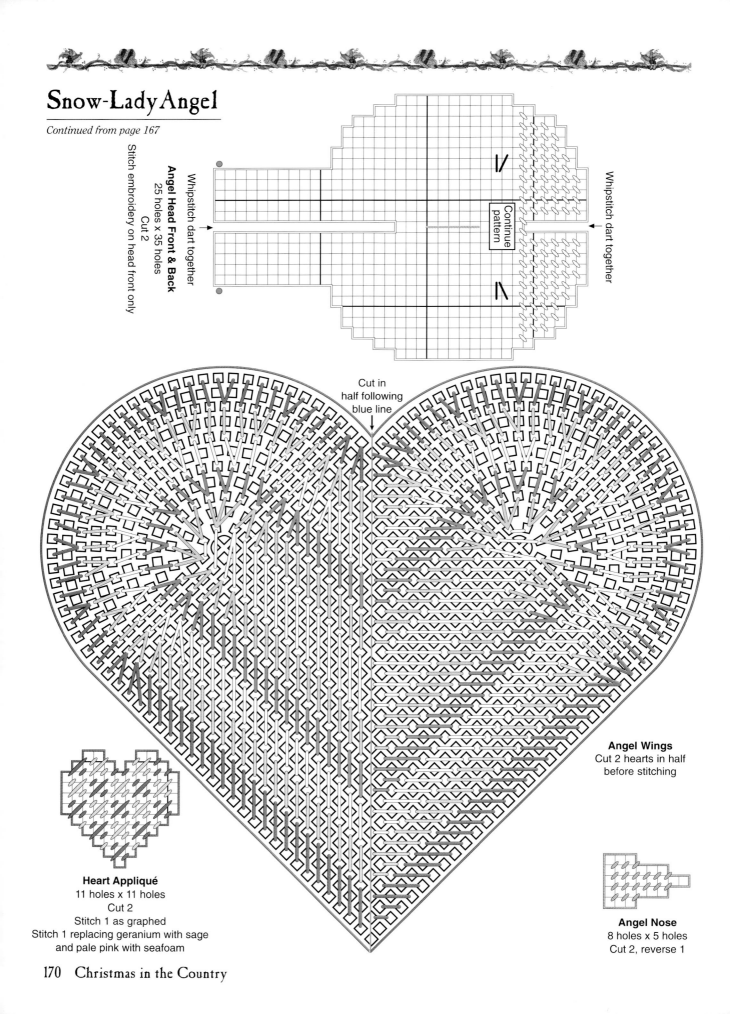

Angel Head Front & Back
25 holes x 35 holes
Cut 2
Stitch embroidery on head front only

Whipstitch dart together

Whipstitch dart together

Continue pattern

Cut in half following blue line

Angel Wings
Cut 2 hearts in half before stitching

Heart Appliqué
11 holes x 11 holes
Cut 2
Stitch 1 as graphed
Stitch 1 replacing geranium with sage and pale pink with seafoam

Angel Nose
8 holes x 5 holes
Cut 2, reverse 1

Sweet Country Angel

*Decked in a charming gingham dress, this curly-haired darling
is always a welcome addition to one's holiday decor!*

Skill Level
Beginner

Materials
- 2 sheets 7-count plastic canvas
- Spinrite Bernat Berella "4" worsted weight yarn as listed in color key
- #16 tapestry needle
- Ceramic buttons from Mill Hill Products by Gay Bowles Sales, Inc.:
  Red heart #86009
  2 gingermen with hearts #86156
- ⅜" red 4-hole button
- Sewing needle and thread or floss to match buttons
- Small amount strawberry blonde #06-300 MiniCurl™ doll hair by One & Only Creations
- 7½" white doll stand by Fibre-Craft

Instructions

1. Cut plastic canvas according to graph (page 172). Back will remain unstitched.

2. Stitch piece following graph. Work Backstitches and French Knots with 2 plies yarn.

3. Using sewing needle and matching thread or floss and following graph throughout, sew heart button at neck, ⅜" red button for holly berry by leaves and gingermen to apron.

4. Overcast bottom edge of front from dot to dot with honey. Whipstitch remaining edges of front to back following graph.

5. Glue small amount of doll hair over hair area on angel front. Remove ring portion at top of doll stand. Insert stand in angel.

Designed by Joan Green

Special Thanks

*We'd like to give a special thank you to each of the following designers whose
work is featured in this delightful collection of country Christmas designs.
This book would not have been possible without them!*

Louise Arganbright
Country Hearts Basket

Angie Arickx
Christmas Quilt Table Ensemble,
Gingerbread Wreath, Mock-Knit Stockings,
Poinsettia Bread Basket, Santa's Workshop,
Whimsical Elf Doorstop

Vicki Blizzard
Baby Animals, Beary Christmas,
Happy Ho-Ho Days, Peppermint Candy
Bluebird, Santa & Snowman Surprise
Boxes, Silhouette Cardinal Candlesticks,
Snow-Lady Angel

**Celia Lange & Martha Bleidner of
Celia Lange Designs**
Christmas Countdown Tree, Christmas
Goose Centerpiece, Christmas Remembered,
Christmas Rose Pin, Country Baskets,
Country Buffet Helpers, Heart-to-Heart

Accessories, Mini Mittens, Mini Toys, Quilt
Block Ornament, Reindeer Match Holder,
Snowman Carolers, Snowman Family,
Welcome Wreath, Winter Luminaries

Mary T. Cosgrove
Pet Goodie Keepers

Dianne Davis
Pocketful of Posies

Darla Fanton
Icicle Santas

Conn Baker Gibney
Poinsettia Tissue Topper

Joan Green
Elegant Mantel Runner, Fireplace Photo
Frame, Folk Country Stockings,
Gingerbread Cookie Tin, Jolly St. Nick,
Sweet Country Angel, We Believe in Santa

Judi Kauffman
My Pals Photo Frame

Kristine Loffredo
Santa Magnet

Karen McDanel
Handy Stocking Hangers

Michele Wilcox
Blossoms & Lace, Christmas Cat,
Christmas Journal, Comfort & Joy,
Country Snowmen, Elfin Santas, Festive
Gift Boxes, I ♥ Snowmen, Merry Little
Christmas, Santa Photo Frame

Kathy Wirth
Home Is Where the Heart Is

Linda Wyszynski
Christmas Tree Coasters,
Friendship Bookmarks

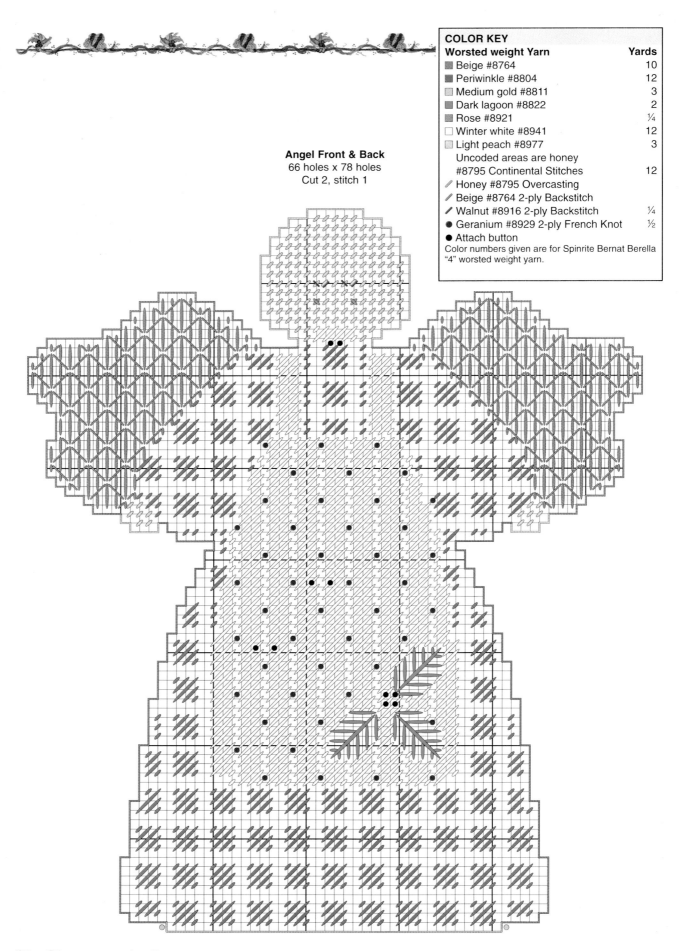

Angel Front & Back
66 holes x 78 holes
Cut 2, stitch 1

Stitch Guide

Use the following diagrams to expand your plastic canvas stitching skills. For each diagram, bring needle up through canvas at the red number one and go back down through the canvas at the red number two. The second stitch is numbered in green. Always bring needle up through the canvas at odd numbers and take it back down through the canvas at the even numbers.

Background Stitches

The following stitches are used for filling in large areas of canvas. The Continental Stitch is the most commonly used stitch. Other stitches, such as the Condensed Mosaic and Scotch Stitch, fill in large areas of canvas more quickly than the Continental Stitch because their stitches cover a larger area of canvas.

Continental Stitch

Condensed Mosaic
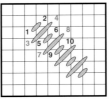

Running Stitch
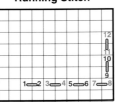

Cross Stitch
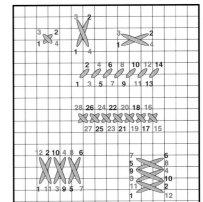

Long Stitch

Slanting Gobelin

Scotch Stitch

Embroidery Stitches

Embroidery stitches are worked on top of a stitched area to add detail and beauty to your project. Embroidery stitches are usually worked with one strand of yarn, several strands of pearl cotton or several strands of embroidery floss.

Lattice Stitch
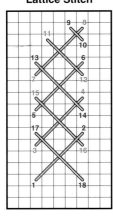

Chain Stitch
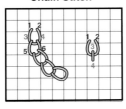

Straight Stitch
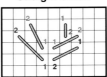

Fly Stitch

Couching
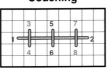

Backstitch
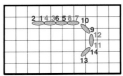

Embroidery Stitches

French Knot

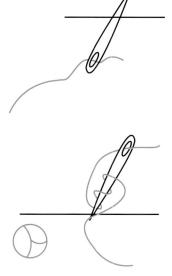

Bring needle up through piece.

Wrap yarn around needle 2 or 3 times, depending on desired size of knot; take needle back through piece through same hole.

Lazy Daisy

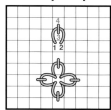

Bring yarn needle up through canvas, then back down in same hole, leaving a small loop.

Then, bring needle up inside loop; take needle back down through piece on other side of loop.

Loop Stitch or Turkey Loop Stitch

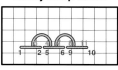

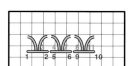

The top diagram shows this stitch left intact. This is an effective stitch for giving a project dimensional hair. The bottom diagram demonstrates the cut loop stitch. Because each stitch is anchored, cutting it will not cause the stitches to come out. A group of cut loop stitches gives a fluffy, soft look and feel to your project.

Specialty Stitches

The following stitches can be worked either on top of a previously stitched area or directly onto the canvas. Like the embroidery stitches, these too add wonderful detail and give your stitching additional interest and texture.

Diamond Eyelet

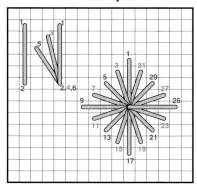

For each stitch, bring needle up at odd numbers around outside and take needle down through canvas at center hole.

Smyrna Cross

Satin Stitch

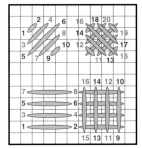

This stitch gives a "padded" look to your work.

Finishing Stitches

Both of these stitches are used to finish the outer edges of the canvas. Overcasting is done to finish one edge at a time. Whipstitch is used to stitch two pieces of canvas together. For both Overcasting and Whipstitching, work one stitch in each hole along straight edges and inside corners, and two or three stitches in outside corners.

Overcast/Whipstitch

Index